"Few books are so needed as this. Recapturing the vision of the pastor as scholar and the scholar as pastor is crucial for the health of the church. Who would not want to read John Piper and D. A. Carson as they reflect on this calling? This is one of the most encouraging and helpful books I have seen in a long time. If you are a pastor, read it. If you have a pastor, put it in his hands."

R. Albert Mohler Jr., President, The Southern Baptist Theological Seminary

"These are important chapters by two of evangelicalism's most important thinkers. In an age that has largely forgotten the native connection between theology and the church, Piper and Carson remind us that these two worlds belong together. There can be, of course, no turning back the clock; the modern research university is here to stay. But here they offer us two good examples of how to navigate the contemporary terrain with a view to producing *ecclesial theology*—theology in service to the church. This short book is a great beginning to a conversation that has been long overdue."

Gerald Hiestand, Senior Associate Pastor, Calvary Memorial Church, Oak Park, Illinois; Executive Director, Society for the Advancement of Ecclesial Theology

"Who could count how many of us have had our lives changed by the ministries of John Piper and D. A. Carson? How many more have come to Christ or have been discipled in the gospel by pastors and teachers influenced by these leaders? This book is a riveting breed, granting us a candid, personal, and behind-the-scenes look at what the Lord has used to shape these men and their ministries. As you read this book, pray that the Lord Jesus would raise up, even now, the next generation of pastor-theologians and theologian-pastors to carry on the great work of Christ exaltation and kingdom mission."

Russell D. Moore, Dean, The Southern Baptist Theological Seminary

"How we need pastors and professors who love God with their minds and their emotions. Two of the preeminent evangelicals of our day reflect here on what it means to love Christ with all our heart. I was encouraged, convicted, and challenged by this book. It is a treasure well worth reading and rereading."

Thomas R. Schreiner, James Buchanan Harrison Professor of New Testament Interpretation, The Southern Baptist Theological Seminary

"I'm deeply encouraged by the growing number of pastoral scholars and scholarly pastors. Probably no living Christians have done more to bring about this trend than D. A. Carson and John Piper. In this book, they will inspire you with stories from their journeys and challenge you with seasoned advice. Most of all, they will lead you to thank God that he gives you the privilege of leading and teaching his church."

Collin Hansen, Editorial Director, The Gospel Coalition; coauthor, *A God-Sized Vision: Revival Stories that Stretch and Stir*

The Pastor as Scholar
&
the Scholar as Pastor

The Pastor as Scholar

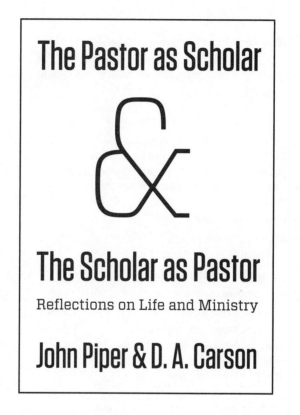

The Scholar as Pastor

Reflections on Life and Ministry

John Piper & D. A. Carson

edited by Owen Strachan & David Mathis

 **CROSSWAY**

WHEATON, ILLINOIS

The Pastor as Scholar and the Scholar as Pastor:
Reflections on Life and Ministry

Cover design: Josh Dennis

Cover photo: Bill Walsh

First printing 2011

Printed in the United States of America

Scripture quotations marked AT are the author's translation.

All emphases in Scripture have been added by the authors.

Trade paperback ISBN: 978-1-4335-2647-3
PDF ISBN: 978-1-4335-2648-0
Mobipocket ISBN: 978-1-4335-2649-7
ePub ISBN: 978-1-4335-2650-3

Library of Congress Cataloging-in-Publication Data
Piper, John, 1946–
  The pastor as scholar and the scholar as pastor : reflections on life and ministry / John Piper and D. A. Carson; Contributing Editors, David Mathis and Owen Strachan.
      p. cm.
  Includes bibliographical references and index.
  ISBN 978-1-4335-2647-3 (tpb)
  1. Pastoral theology. 2. Theology—Study and teaching.
3. Clergy—Post-ordination training. I. Carson, D. A.
II. Mathis, David, 1980–   . III. Strachan, Owen. IV. Title.
BV4011.3.P58   2011
253.071'5—dc22   2010045336

Crossway is a publishing ministry of Good News Publishers.

LB		21	20	19	18	17	16	15	14	13	12	11
13	12	11	10	9	8	7	6	5	4	3	2	1

To

Harold John Ockenga (1905–1985)
pastor, writer, seminary founder

and

Carl F. H. Henry (1913–2003)
theologian, writer/editor, churchman

Remember your leaders,
those who spoke to you the word of God.
Consider the outcome of their way of life,
and imitate their faith.
Jesus Christ is the same
yesterday and today and forever.
—Hebrews 13:7–8

Contents

Acknowledgments   11

Introduction   13
The Return of the Pastor-Scholar
Owen Strachan

CHAPTER ONE
The Pastor as Scholar: 21
A Personal Journey and the Joyful Place
of Scholarship
John Piper

CHAPTER TWO
The Scholar as Pastor: 71
Lessons from the Church and the Academy
D. A. Carson

Conclusion   107
The Preacher, the Professor, and the True
Pastor-Scholar
David Mathis

Notes   113

General Index   117

Scripture Index   123

Acknowledgments

Before it was a book, *The Pastor as Scholar and the Scholar as Pastor* was originally a single-evening event sponsored by the Carl F. H. Henry Center for Theological Understanding at Trinity Evangelical Divinity School, held on Thursday, April 23, 2009, at Park Community Church in Chicago. We thank Doug Sweeney, Director of the Henry Center; Jackson Crum, J. R. Kerr, Joe Riccardi, and Whitney Anderson of Park Community Church; Ben Peays of The Gospel Coalition; and the title sponsor of the event, BibleMesh.com.

We also thank John Piper and Don Carson for their willingness to add this event to an already full week of meetings with The Gospel Coalition, as well as for putting their messages to paper and investing the extra energy to expand the original versions into these chapters.

Thank you to our wives, Megan Mathis and Bethany Strachan, who didn't begrudge our initial phone conversations or the time it took to bring this book together and guide it through the editorial process—Bethany, in addition to caring for Owen while he was injured, and Megan, in addition to carrying the twin boys toward their summer 2010 due date.

Most importantly, we thank Jesus, in a sense the true pastor-scholar. May all praise and glory and honor and power be his.

David Mathis, Minneapolis, Minnesota
Owen Strachan, Deerfield, Illinois
June 1, 2010

Introduction
The Return of the Pastor-Scholar

Owen Strachan

"What do you want to be—a pastor or a scholar?"

It's a common question in some circles. Many young leaders-in-training have wrestled with its binary nature. *I must*, they think to themselves with some anguish, *be one or the other. Surely I cannot be both.* So the wrestling begins and uneasy conversations follow. For many, tidy resolutions prove evasive.

Perhaps it isn't meant to be so. What if the question, though well intended, suffers from a potentially fatal flaw? What if—hold your breath—one could be *both*? What then?

This book stems from more than a sneaking suspicion that this rather mischievous counter-question might be onto something. This suspicion does not proceed from a vacuum but from the history of God's church. Unlike our more recent history, when pastors were urged by some to busy themselves with the pragmatic matters of everyday ministry and some scholars focused less on the church and more on high-level academic questions, pastors and scholars throughout the larger span of church history have blended these roles. Pastors worked out of a burden to bless their people with rich biblical theology even as scholars labored to nourish, strengthen, and captivate the church through their scholarship. Often the roles of pastor and scholar were filled by the same person. The pastor was a scholar; the scholar was a pastor.

This is particularly true of the Reformed tradition, the guild whose trans-denominational movement continues to grow in the current day. In Augustine, Luther, Calvin, many Puritans, Edwards, Spurgeon, Lloyd-Jones, and many more, we find men who loved the church and excelled as theologians. Though our more modern binary categories of "pastor only" and "scholar only" might *seem* justified, when one turns to the actual history of the church, one finds countless examples of the scholarly pastor and the pastoral scholar. Neither role is a cop-out; both require that their adherents perform all the usual duties of the biblical local church pastor and teacher. We must not make the mistake of making evangelism the enemy of theology, discipleship the enemy of edifying scholarship. Whether in the form of a Calvin, an Edwards, or many others, this simply does not ring true. These examples reveal that robust theology, so far from hindering the practice of ministry, actually enriches it, even as the practice of ministry enhances and increases one's appreciation for theology.

These models of pastor and scholar thrive in the current day, contrary to what some might think. John Piper and D. A. Carson are two of evangelicalism's best-known figures. Each has provided leadership for the movement in distinct ways. From his iconic position at Bethlehem Baptist Church, Piper has modeled the theologically minded pastor. Throughout his long and distinguished career at

Trinity Evangelical Divinity School, Carson has exemplified the ecclesially concerned scholar. Each man has published dozens of books, marking them as a leading voice for evangelicals of varying backgrounds. Both have published on a variety of levels, whether for popular, churchly, or scholarly reading.

The giftings of each man have rendered them an example for fellow ministry leaders and believers. Because they have proved able to speak both clearly and profoundly, and always with a sovereign God and a salvific gospel in view, Piper and Carson represent a contemporary starting point for a much wider discussion of ministerial calling.

It was for this constellation of reasons that the Carl F. H. Henry Center for Theological Understanding at Trinity Evangelical Divinity School asked Drs. Piper and Carson to speak at a special event geared toward future pastors and scholars on April 23, 2009. Coming on the heels of The Gospel Coalition national conference, the event was entitled "The Pastor as Scholar, the Scholar as Pastor: Reflections on Life and Ministry with John Piper and D. A. Carson." It attracted a capacity crowd to Park Community Church in downtown Chicago. The auditorium and two floors of overflow classrooms were filled with attendees who had come to hear the two leaders speak on their callings. For three hours, the audience listened to the scholarly pastor and the pastoral scholar. Thousands more streamed the media after the event, which created quite a buzz on numerous blogs and other forms of social media.[1]

This book, we hope, serves the growing conversation

on the identities of ministry callings. In addition to the aforementioned event, the Society for the Advancement of Ecclesial Theology, based in the Chicago area, convened in 2007 and is bursting with applications from interested pastors who have a concern to engage the life of the mind in their pastoral work. Theologian Kevin J. Vanhoozer gave the Page Lectures at Southeastern Baptist Theological Seminary in late 2009 and commented at length on the necessity of the pastor-theologian, evangelicalism's "public intellectual" according to Vanhoozer.[2] On the publishing front, R. Albert Mohler Jr.'s *He Is Not Silent* includes a chapter on the pastor as theologian.[3] David Wells's *The Courage to Be Protestant* argues that historically, "scholar–saints" led the church, pastors who were "as comfortable with books and learning as with the aches of the soul."[4] Douglas Sweeney's *Jonathan Edwards and the Ministry of the Word* includes important content about Edwards's ministry as a pastor-theologian.[5] An insightful article on the topic by Gerald Hiestand ran in the *Westminster Journal of Theology* in 2008.[6] The recent systematic theology for the church by Daniel Akin, *A Theology for the Church*, features chapters by leading theologians and scholarly pastors that are aimed at the local church and its leaders.[7] In these and other texts, Christian thinkers are mulling over an enhanced pastorate and an engaged academia.

The Pastor as Scholar and the Scholar as Pastor serves as a short, readable introduction to these callings. It suggests by way of experience and meditation an answer to the question posed earlier: "What do you want to be—a pastor or a scholar?" Perhaps we will be forgiven if, like Pastor Piper and Professor Carson, we want in some small way to be a realistic combination of both, in order that we might use our gifts in service to God for the health of our brothers and sisters. This, and no mere rearrangement of ministerial furniture, is the aim of this text: the strengthening of God's church for the greater glory of its Lord.

The Pastor as Scholar

CHAPTER ONE

The Pastor as Scholar: A Personal Journey and the Joyful Place of Scholarship

John Piper

This chapter has two parts. First is the story of my pilgrimage to the pastorate, and second is the way "scholarship" relates to the overarching theme of my ministry—that God is most glorified in us when we are most satisfied in him. The story I tell, from the time I was a boy in high school to the stage in life where I am now, has an angle to it, namely, highlighting the factors along the way that shaped me into the kind of pastor I am today, for good or for ill. The very fact that I am approaching the topic of pastor-scholar this way is immediately part of what you should learn about what makes me tick as a pastor, and how this relates to scholarship. Don't hold your breath waiting for me to say something about making room for academic scholarship in the busy life of a pastor.

Part One: The Making of a Pastor-Scholar

From one angle this approach is typically American—we Americans, in general, more quickly bare our souls to the world than many cultures do. For example, F. F. Bruce, representing the British of a generation ago (and perhaps much like today's), said at the end of his autobiography:

> While some readers have observed that in these chapters I have said little about my domestic life, others have wondered why I have been so reticent about my religious experience. The reason is probably the same in both instances: I do not care to speak much—especially in public—about the things that mean most to me. Others do not share this inhibition, and have enriched their fellows by relating the inner story of the Lord's dealings with them—one thinks of Augustine's *Confessions* and Bunyan's *Grace Abounding*. But it calls for quite exceptional qualities to be able to do this kind of thing without self-consciousness or self-deception.[1]

So now you can see I am trapped. My first reaction when I read this was to say, "No wonder I have found his commentaries so dry"—helpful in significant ways, but personally and theologically anemic. My second reaction was to say (this was in 1980, the year I left academia and entered the pastorate), "Good grief! You say, 'I do not care to speak much—especially in public—about the things that mean most to me.' I say, 'The *only* thing I care to speak about—especially in public—are the things that mean most to me!'"

Zero Empathy

Both his and my statements are probably overstatements. But seriously, this is one of the differences between me and many scholars, and it is part of what pushed me out of the guild. I am regularly bursting to say something about the

most precious things in the universe—and not in any disin-
terested, dispassionate, composed, detached, unemotional,
so-called scholarly way, but rather with total interest, warm
passion, discomposure, utter attachment, and fully emotional, and, I hope always, *true*. At least *true* is my goal.

I am with Jonathan Edwards all the way when he says:

> I should think myself in the way of my duty to raise the
> affections of my hearers as high as possibly I can, pro-
> vided that they are affected with nothing but truth, and
> with affections that are not disagreeable to the nature of
> what they are affected with.[2]

Of course, my assumption is, for Edwards and for myself,
that in our aim to raise the affections of our hearers, we
have experienced authentically raised affections ourselves.
And these affections are in synch with what is true and in
proportion to the nature of the truth.

So I have zero empathy with F. F. Bruce and others when
they say (sometimes in the name of personality, and others
in the name of scholarly objectivity), "I do not care to speak
much—especially in public—about the things that mean
most to me." Nor do I care if they say a theological lecture
or a critical scholarly commentary is not the place for that.

But now you can see that he has me trapped, because he
says, "Others do not share this inhibition, and have enriched
their fellows by relating the inner story of the Lord's deal-
ings with them—one thinks of Augustine's *Confessions* and
Bunyan's *Grace Abounding*. But it calls for quite exceptional
qualities to be able to do this kind of thing without self-

consciousness or self-deception." So, to follow the course I have set for myself, I must think myself in the possession of "exceptional qualities" and perhaps be in the ranks of Augustine and Bunyan! What shall I do?

There is another possibility—in fact, there are several. One is that I do not have "exceptional qualities," and I may just be stupid to take this approach. Another possibility is that I may be egotistical and vain. The Internet world we live in today is awash in narcissism and vanity, with some people taking their clothes off literally, because exposure gives them a rush, and others doing it spiritually—because the addicting power of talking about yourself, where anyone in the world can read it, is overpowering.

I put Philippians 2:3 before me regularly with its piercing word *kenodoxian* (vainglory): "Do nothing from rivalry or vainglory [*kenodoxian*], but in humility count others more significant than yourselves" (Phil. 2:3 AT). The love of human praise—human glory—is universal and deadly.

Jesus said, "How can you believe, when you receive glory from one another and do not seek the glory that comes from the only God?" (John 5:44).[3] You can't. You can't believe in the crucified Messiah as your supreme treasure and hero, and then love the exact opposite of the mind-set that took him to the cross.

So, in pursuing an autobiographical approach in this chapter, I may be stupid, or I may be vain. Or another possibility is that I may be Pauline.

> We do not want you to be ignorant, brothers, of the
> affliction we experienced in Asia. For we were so utterly

burdened beyond our strength that we despaired of life itself. Indeed, we felt that we had received the sentence of death. But that was to make us rely not on ourselves but on God who raises the dead. (2 Cor. 1:8–9)

I want you to know how great a struggle I have for you and for those at Laodicea and for all who have not seen me face to face, that their hearts may be encouraged. (Col. 2:1–2)

I want you to know, brothers, that what has happened to me has really served to advance the gospel, so that it has become known throughout the whole imperial guard and to all the rest that my imprisonment is for Christ. (Phil. 1:12–13)

In other words, Paul repeatedly talks about his personal life and experience with God with a view to helping his listeners. So, yes, this approach is risky. But there are reasons for it.

Maybe I'm Not One

One of my reasons involves a huge assumption. I assume that one of the main reasons I was asked to contribute to this book with Don Carson is that somebody thinks I am one of these—a pastor-scholar. Depending on the definition, I'm not sure I am. And so I thought maybe I should tell my story about how I got to be the way I am, and you could decide if I am or not. Or *in what sense* I am or am not. And if that's a good thing or not. And what the implications are for you and for the church.

So I'm going to look at six chapters of my life through the lens of this question: What were the impulses toward scholarship and the pastorate? And along the way you will pick up on what I mean by *scholarship* and *pastoring*.

Early Youth

When I was six years old at a motel in Florida on vacation with my family, I prayed with my mother and affirmed my faith in Jesus as my Savior. My parents were Christians, and my father was an evangelist. I loved them, admired them, and embraced the truth that they taught me. The influence of my father was huge, and I admired him as a preacher.

But very quickly I knew that I would never be a preacher because by the time I was in junior high school, I could not speak in front of any group. I was paralyzed with anxiety about it and trembled so terribly and choked up so completely that it was physically impossible to read or speak before any size group. Don't imagine your average person with butterflies. Imagine physical impossibility. So preaching and the pastorate were totally ruled out of my dreams.

Moreover, there was no apparent vision for *scholarship* in my home. It was not even a category in our minds, or a word in our vocabulary. My father had a library and a study at home, but I never thought about it. I saw my father's Greek New Testament, but I never saw him use it or heard him refer to using it—though I noted that it was marked up and that it was used once upon a time.

So *pastoring* was not an option because of my disability (or whatever it was), and *scholarship* was a nonexistent category when I went to high school. But I was a believer. I loved Jesus. I hated sin. I feared God in a good way. I took heaven and hell and salvation and the gospel very seriously. They were dominant realities in my life. And so the seeds of ministry were there. But there was no dream to be a pastor and no awareness that there even was such a thing as scholarship.

High School Days

In high school, there was a double awakening; one was intellectual and the other was emotional and expressive. On the intellectual side, there was advanced biology and tenth-grade geometry. These stand out as very significant.

The process of reasoning from axioms and postulates and corollaries in order to turn theories into proofs was explosively exciting to me. I loved the ability to draw right conclusions from true premises. Geometry class marked a serious awakening of my love for right thinking. From that time to this, I have had an ear and an eye for non sequiturs in what I hear and read. If a politician or preacher says, "All cows have four legs; Fido has four legs; therefore Fido is a cow," I'm all over it. From that class on, I have had a self-conscious expectation that I will never knowingly be illogical or incoherent.

Then there was Mrs. Clanton's advanced biology class where we dissected worms and frogs and fetal pigs and bred tsetse flies. Many of you have heard the story of Agassiz's Fish,[4] about the naturalist who demanded of his student that he sit and stare at a fish for a week to learn all he could. Well,

Mrs. Clanton was like that. The point of all this dissection was to awaken in us the crucial discipline of accurate and thorough observation. Do you see what's really in the pig? All the sharp reasoning in the world will simply lead you astray if you start with observations that are inaccurate or incomplete.

It was no surprise to me then in seminary when Agassiz's Fish was used in a hermeneutics class,[5] and when in Germany I read the New Testament scholar Adolf Schlatter, "Die Wissenschaft ist erstens Beobachtung, zweitens Beobachtung, drittens Beobachtung" ("Science/scholarship is first observation, second observation, third observation"). So what happened in Mrs. Clanton's biology class was the awakening of a self-conscious awareness that dependable knowledge—of the world or the Bible or anything else—depends on seeing what's really there for the mind to work with.

These were two huge impulses feeding into who I am in ministry: painstaking observation of texts and the demand for precise thinking—from myself and from others.

Two other awakenings in high school have never gone away. One was the passion to write, and the other was the bent toward poetry. My father sowed the seeds of poetry, because he wrote poems for special occasions, and he read poems to the family. Even in the months before his death at 87, I would ask him to read his poems to me, and he would weep at certain points as he read about his six-year-old son.

But all of that lay dormant until the spring of 1963 during my junior year. In my English class, the desire to read serious books and the desire to write serious essays and poems was born. This has never gone away. Writing has been an almost daily habit since then—in one form or another—notes, letters, journal entries, poems, ideas, reports, essays, sermons, and more.

Writing became the lever of my thinking and the outlet of my feelings. If I didn't pull the lever, the wheel of thinking did not turn. It jerked and squeaked and halted. But once a pen was in hand, or a keyboard, the fog began to clear and the wheel of thought began to spin with more clarity and insight. And when the feelings that rumbled around in my heart as an introverted, insecure adolescent needed form, I turned to poetry and writing. So along with the disciplines of precise thinking and painstaking observation came a passion for conceptually clear and emotionally moving expression in writing.

Two last things remain to be underlined about high school. I knew when I was done that I could not speak in front of any group, and I was deeply troubled and anxious about my future—what kind of job would help me avoid that? And I knew also that I read painfully slowly. To this day, I cannot read faster than I can talk. Something short-circuits in my ability to perceive accurately what's on the page, when I try to push beyond that—probably some form of dyslexia. Those two disabilities, paralysis before people and painfully slow reading, I knew would keep me out of any profession that demanded great quantities of reading and any public speaking.

But Jesus was real to me. I turned to him in my sorrows. I loved my church. I hated sin. I feared God. I believed in the

Bible and in heaven and hell. Somehow, my life had to count. But I did not know how.

Wheaton College

The season at Wheaton was enormously influential in fanning the flames that had been lit in high school—the intellectual stimulation, the emotional deepening, the passion to write. In one sense, my college and seminary days relate to each other as form and substance. The college days solidified passions and habits of mind; the seminary days defined what the focus of those habits would be, namely, God and his Word and his people.

The influences of these days can be grouped under the mind, the heart, the synthesis, and the bridge to ministry.

Mind

Arthur Holmes and Stuart Hackett were both in the philosophy department at Wheaton in the late sixties. Holmes embodied two things I had never seen before: (1) the quest for a comprehensive worldview that helped make sense of everything—and that had Christ as the integrating center—and (2) the life of the mind as vocation. In other words, Christian scholarship as a vocation came onto my horizon as a possibility for the first time in my life.

Stuart Hackett was probably one of the two most influential teachers I had at Wheaton, not because of the theology he held but because of the way he thought. I had only two classes with him, and the content of every class session seemed to me to be the same—and never boring. He was the philosophical embodiment of what geometry had meant to me in the tenth grade.

The point of every class seemed to be: any system of thought that denies truth denies itself. In other words, he modeled the universal significance of the law of noncontradiction: if you say there's no truth, then you've just spoken something that doesn't count. That simple insight has been life-saving and life-illuminating for over forty years. It spared me from being enamored by all the ludicrous postmodernism that was already rampant in the late 1960s. Thank you, Dr. Hackett.

Francis Schaeffer burst on the scene in the fall of 1965 and had the effect of taking all the intellectual awakening and showing us that it could be culturally and evangelistically engaging. In other words, he seemed to embody a way of taking all the scholarly impulses of the ivory tower and putting them to personal and social use for the sake of Christ in the world. So his particular way of doing apologetics had the effect of helping many of us believe that the intellectual awakening we were experiencing at Wheaton could really be a blessing in the world more broadly than we thought.

Another influence at Wheaton was the students. Never had I been around so many intellectually engaged young people. It had a double effect. One was to pour gasoline on the fires lit by the professors. The other was to remind me of my weaknesses. Because of this kind of expectation in the classroom, I was not an outstanding student at Wheaton. My GPA, if I remember correctly was what today would be about a 3.2. I was a B student, not an A student. Therefore, I never thought of myself as becoming a front-ranking anything. I was not superior in any way at Wheaton.

Heart

Along with these intellectual springs bubbling up, there was another river flowing. My love of reading and writing led me to be a literature major. The literature faculty was renowned. I took every poetry class that Wheaton offered. And I avoided every novel class that was offered. I could not read fast enough to get through the novels in a semester, but I could write and analyze poetry. So I carefully navigated my way through a lit major as one of the slowest readers on campus.

Mainly poetry was chosen because the emotions of a young man can run deep in the river of poetry. Clyde Kilby was a giant in the lit department in those days, and his book *Poetry and Life* was lived in front of us in class. Kilby took the passion for observation and breathed a kind of life into it that biology never could. He taught me that there is always more to see in what I see. There is always wonder. There is always something to be astonished about. There is mental health in learning to look at a tree or a cloud or a nose, and to marvel that it is what it is. This then became poetry. When you finally see the wonder of what you have been looking at for ten years, what you do with that seeing is try to say it—and that is what poetry is.

One of his resolutions for being a healthy person reads like this:

I shall open my eyes and ears. Once every day, I shall simply stare at a tree, a flower, a cloud, a person. I shall not then be concerned at all to ask what they are, but simply be glad that they are. I shall joyfully allow them the mystery of what Lewis calls, "their divine, magical, terrifying, and ecstatic existence."[6]

When you are being shown what you've always looked at all your life and never seen, it is absolutely revolutionary. Kilby was one of the greatest influences of my life, and I scarcely know what he thought about anything—politically, psychologically, theologically. It was the *way* he saw the world and spoke of the world. He was so alive to the wonder of things. This was incalculably valuable preparation of soul for the vision of God that would come just a few years later at seminary.

In this section on heart belongs Noël Henry. She has been my wife for over forty years. But in those days, starting in the summer of 1966, she was this ravishing object of desire. Oh, how I wanted to be married to Noël. Falling in love is very powerful. Not in vain does the Song of Solomon say, "I adjure you, O daughters of Jerusalem, that you not stir up or awaken love until it pleases" (Song 8:4). The effects of finding a wife are so pervasive and long lasting that they are immeasurable, so here is where she entered my life, and nothing has been the same since. I owe her more than anyone else in the world.

Synthesis

The synthesis of mind and heart was embodied in C. S. Lewis. Lewis became for me in my college days what Jonathan Edwards became in my seminary days—a towering figure of intellectual and emotional influence. He was a "romantic rationalist"—that was the name of a small book about Lewis that got me very excited because it summed up what I thought I was (which may be very akin to "pastor-scholar"). His influence on me is great and varied.

Lewis embodied the fact that rigorous, precise, penetrating logic is not inimical to deep, soul-stirring feeling and vivid, lively—even playful—imagination. He combined what almost everybody today assumes are mutually exclusive: rationalism and poetry, cool logic and warm feeling, disciplined prose and free imagination. In shattering these old stereotypes for me, he freed me to think hard and to write poetry, to argue for the resurrection and compose hymns to Christ, to smash an argument and hug a friend, to demand a definition and use a metaphor.

Lewis was the main influence on Clyde Kilby, and Lewis had the same effect on me as Kilby did. He gave me an intense sense of the "realness" of things. To wake up in the morning and be aware of the firmness of the mattress, the warmth of the sun rays, the sound of the clock ticking, the sheer being of things ("quiddity" as he called it). He helped me become alive to life. He helped me see what is there in the world—things which if we didn't have, we would pay a million dollars to have, but having them, ignore.

Finally, he has made me wary of chronological snobbery.

That is, he has shown me that "newness" is no virtue and "oldness" is no fault. Truth and beauty and goodness are not determined by when they exist. Nothing is inferior for being old, and nothing is valuable for being modern. This has freed me from the tyranny of novelty.

These were immeasurable gifts and had the effect of synthesizing my Wheaton experience. The intellectual stimulation, the emotional deepening, the stirring of imagination, the passion to write—all of these came together in C. S. Lewis and made me wonder if I should teach English literature as a vocation.[7]

The Bridge to Ministry

There were other key factors that God was putting in place that were going to determine the direction all this energy would take. I'll mention four. Together these are the bridge that God built to seminary and the ministry of the Word.

First came the momentous summer of '66. Not only did I meet Noël, but chaplain Evan Welsh asked me to pray in summer school chapel. For reasons I cannot recall or imagine, I said yes. That meant standing in front of about five hundred students and faculty and praying for about one minute (maximum). Never in my life had I been able to do such a thing in front of ten, let alone five hundred. I vowed to God on front campus: *If you will get me through this without my choking and becoming paralyzed, I will never again say no to a speaking opportunity out of fear.* He answered that prayer, and I believe something broke. And I think I have kept my vow.

Harold John Ockenga came to preach in chapel in the fall of 1966. I was lying in the campus health center with mono as I listened to him on the radio. And God created in my heart at that time a desire to study and understand and teach the Word of God that has never died. It is as alive and strong today as it ever was. So the bridge to seminary was being built. I was on my way to a clear biblical focus for all the intellect and emotion and imagination and writing that were being awakened and deepened at Wheaton.

Then came John Stott and *Men Made New*, a little yellow paperback of an exposition of Romans 5–8. I loved it. It was fuel on the flame that Ockenga had lit, and it showed me the kind of careful attention to the text that, for me, made it live.

Then came Urbana '67 where Stott again opened 2 Timothy in a week of messages and where the utter indispensability of global missions hit home.

With all of that (the anxiety breakthrough, the call of God through Ockenga, the modeling of John Stott, the impulse of missions), the bridge was built to pursue the study of God's Word in seminary. I did not know what I would do with it vocationally. All I knew is that everything that God had done in my life was getting me ready to study his Word and somehow use it for the church and missions.

Fuller Seminary

When I went to Fuller, I was detached from the local church. In college I had not seriously engaged with one local church. That was foolish and immature. It continued for a few months in seminary, and then I got married and knew I needed to grow up. Noël and I went to Lake Avenue Congregational Church where Ray Ortlund Sr. was the senior pastor. There we fell in love with the church—the local church of real people with real relationships. By the time we were done, Noël was caring for the mentally disabled, and I had taught seventh grade, ninth grade, and young marrieds. We were in five different small groups. Eventually, four years after I left to go to graduate school, I was ordained at that church. Never again did I play fast and loose with my attachment to the local church. To cut yourself off from a local church with a sense of self-sufficiency is, in the long run, suicidal.

In seminary, explosive things were happening in my soul. I was watching the agony and the ecstasy of the new evangelicalism struggling to break free from the anti-intellectualism and cultural distance of fundamentalism into an intellectual and cultural engagement that would be respected in the guild. Some of these men paid with their lives and their families and their health in the struggle to find scholarly credibility. George Ladd was almost undone emotionally and professionally by a critical review of his *Jesus and the Kingdom* by Norman Perrin of the University of Chicago. And when his *New Testament Theology* was a stunning success ten years later, he walked through the halls shouting and waving a $9,000 royalty check.

The scholarly discipline of Geoffrey Bromiley, who translated all of Kittle's *Theological Dictionary of the New Testament*, was awe-inspiring. But the sophomoric belittling of fundamentalists in some classes by younger faculty was disappointing. This faculty was on a quest to put orthodoxy on the map intellectually. So it was a heady place in the late sixties.

For me it proved to be the most decisive time of my life theologically and methodologically. And the key living person under God was Daniel Fuller. Emotionally and personally, he was as imperfect as the rest of them. (Now I would say, "the rest of *us*.") But in his brokenness, he put so many things together for me.

Nobody thought more rigorously than Dan Fuller. Nobody was more riveted on the biblical text in his exegetical method than Dan Fuller. We called his approach "arcing," and it has been the methodological key for much of what I have seen in the Bible for the past forty years. Nobody was more jealous to think the author's thoughts after him, because that's what meaning was—the author's intention (E. D. Hirsch's *Validity in Interpretation* was compelling).

Nobody was more practically committed to the truth and authority of Scripture than Dan Fuller. Nobody communicated a greater gravity of the ultimate things at stake in biblical truth. Nobody was more vulnerable to students' questions or took them more seriously than Dan Fuller. He would linger for hours after class with us. And he would stay up late writing answers to our questions and then bring the paper the next day to try out his fresh thoughts on us.

Nobody was more committed to showing that much reading is not the essence of scholarship, but that assiduous, detailed, meticulous, logical analysis of great texts can lift you to the level of the greatest minds. Nobody pierced to the essence of true scholarship the way Dan Fuller did. In partnership with Mortimer Adler's *How to Read a Book*, he taught me that the task of the true scholar, whatever his vocation, was:

- to *observe* his subject matter accurately and thoroughly;
- to *understand* clearly what he has observed;
- to *evaluate* fairly what he has understood by deciding what is true and valuable;
- to *feel* intensely according to the value of what he has evaluated;
- to *apply* wisely and helpfully in life what he understands and feels; and
- to *express* in speech and writing and deeds what he has seen, understood, felt, and applied in such a way that its accuracy, clarity, truth, value, and helpfulness can be known and enjoyed by others.

By all of this singularly blood-earnest scholarship, he introduced me, through Scripture and through Jonathan Edwards, to the truth that *God is most glorified in us when I am most satisfied in him*. This was the seed from which has grown all the books I have written and all the sermons I have preached. The fact that God pursued his glory and my joy in the same act of worship was the most explosive truth I have ever learned. The sources were the Bible and then Jonathan Edwards.

I recall the day in class when Fuller was accused of being too rational by a student from the new school of psychology. Fuller responded by saying, "Why can't we be like Jonathan Edwards, who in one moment could be writing a devotion that would warm your grandmother's heart and in the next give a philosophical argument that would stump the chief thinkers of his day?" My heart leaped. I went straight to the library after class, knowing almost nothing of Edwards, and checked out his *Essay on the Trinity*. That's what I read first. Then I bought a stapled photocopy of *The End for Which God Created the World* at the bookstore.

Meanwhile, my exegesis and systematic theology classes were undoing my Arminian presuppositions with biblical facts. By the end of three years, not only was I a romantic rationalist, but the romance and the rational labor were now firmly focused on the Word of God. An absolutely sovereign God of grace was at the center. He had planned the death of his Son for my salvation before the world was made. And if the worst and best things were planned, all was planned. He "works all things according to the counsel of his will" (Eph. 1:11).

All of this was being forged while I was teaching Sunday school, and while I was falling in love with the church under Ray Ortlund's shepherding, and while I was hearing Ralph Winter describe the explosive new realities of missions around the world. Nothing about my emerging theology felt artificial or academic or detached or irrelevant to life. It all felt real and personal and relevant for church and home and the culture and all the nations of the world.

But what to do with my life? The advice I got was, if you have the energy and a wife who's willing, go ahead and get your final degree (a doctorate), and then all the doors will be open to you. So, after I was rejected at Princeton and accepted by Leonhard Goppelt at the University of Munich, we headed for Germany in July 1971.

Doctoral Studies at the University of Munich

What I saw in the theological educational system and state-church life in Germany confirmed most of what I did not want to become. Here were world-class scholars, whom everyone on the cutting edge in America were oohing and ahhing over, teaching in a way that was exegetically non-transferable, insubordinate toward the Scriptures, and indifferent to the life of the church. I attended university classes where nineteen-year-old ministerial students were soaked in every form of faddish criticism, while the tools for mining the gold of Scripture were untouched and the taste buds for enjoying its honey were unawakened.

I recall one appalling illustration of the fruit of this folly. I attended an ordination service where most of the people in the church were older women. The visiting church official stood and announced his text from "Q." I kid you not. If you don't know, "Q" is the scholarly name given to a hypothetical document containing the parts of Matthew and Luke not shared by Mark. I was not impressed with the theological and academic life in Germany in those days.

I wrote my dissertation on Jesus's love command[8] and worshiped in a lively Baptist church and led a small discipleship group every Friday night, and stoked the fires of my faith with Jonathan Edwards and God's Word. But the exegetical methods I saw in Germany could not come close to the theological and methodological goldmine that I had found in seminary. I used my Fuller-taught method of observation and analysis to research and write an acceptable dissertation, and then left Germany as quickly as I could. I did not have to work hard to protect myself from this system. I saw it up close, and from the inside, and found early on that this global king of biblical scholarship had no clothes on.[9]

I was disillusioned with such scholarship. It seemed driven by the need for peer approval. It used technical jargon that only insiders could understand and that often concealed ambiguity. It put enormous weight on speculative methodologies (*Formgeschichte*, *Traditionsgeschichte*, and *Redaktionsgeschichte*, and *Sachkritik*) that gave rise to scholarly articles which began in the mode of *Wahrscheinlichkeit* (probability) and by the end had been transformed into the mode of *Sicherheit* (certainty) by waving the wand of scholarly consensus.

There was the use of linguistic skills to create vagueness and conceal superficiality. Few, it seemed to me, would press the real question of meaning until it yielded the riches of theological truth. The whole enterprise lacked the aroma of heaven or the odor of hell, and there did not seem to be any burden for the lostness of the world.

Exultation over anything glorious was not allowed into their explanations—which meant that the greatest realities were left unexplained, because there are realities that are so great they can only be illumined in the light of exultation. By and large, there seemed to be little apprehension of the incoherence between the infinite value of the object of the study and the naturalistic nature of their study. The whole atmosphere seemed unplugged from the majesty of the object.

I earned my doctorate. They mailed it to me a few months after I left. I took it out of the mailing tube in the fall of 1974 to see if it was real. I put it back in and have not looked at it since. It's still in the tube in a bottom drawer at home (I think), and no one has ever asked to see it. But, by God's grace, it did get me my first job.

Bethel College

I had a wife and child and needed a job. I wrote to about thirty churches, denominations, missions, colleges, and seminaries. One door opened in the fall of 1974 for a one-year sabbatical replacement teaching New Testament at Bethel College in St. Paul, Minnesota. Thank you, Walt Wessel. I took the job and have been in Minnesota ever since.

The one-year sabbatical replacement turned into six happy years teaching New Testament book studies and Greek and New Testament introduction. I thought this was my calling. Be a teacher and a scholar. So I set about to publish my dissertation in the *SNTS Monograph Series*, and I wrote a handful of articles in scholarly journals. These were heady days as I stretched my academic wings. I loved the writing. I loved the teaching.

But gradually things began to change inside of me. God was stirring. I knew I would never be a great scholar. I simply could not read fast enough. I could take a small issue or an article or book and apply the severe discipline of analysis and criticism. But I could not be comprehensive. I could not read all that was written on anything.

Moreover, I was teaching in college, not seminary, and

so the trickledown effect of my teaching for the good of the church had farther to go than if I had been teaching seminary students. That felt frustrating.

I became very restless with the work of grading papers and teaching such a limited slice of the pie of humanity: middle-class, mainly white eighteen- to twenty-two-year-olds. All the while, I was hearing good preaching on Sunday and feeling a fire inside: *Oh, Lord, I would love to do that.* And if I heard a bad sermon, I would feel, *Oh, Lord, we've got to do better than that.*

Then came the sabbatical of May through December 1979. I wrote the book *The Justification of God: An Exegetical and Theological Study of Romans 9:1–23.* While I was living and breathing the air of Romans 9 for eight months, the Lord spoke to me very powerfully through the words of that chapter. He said, in effect, "I, the God of Romans 9, will be *proclaimed* and not just analyzed or explained." By the end of that sabbatical, the battle was over, and I had resolved to leave teaching and seek a pastoral position.

I longed to see the Word of God applied in preaching to the whole range of ages and life situations. I wanted to watch the absolutely sovereign God of Romans 9 build his church. I wanted to see what would happen if the supremacy of God in all things was made the centerpiece of a local church through the Word of God.

I knew what this would mean to leave the world of academia. It would mean no more summers free to read and study and write; endless administrative pressures and challenges; an uncontrollable schedule; an audience who would not want or reward academic prowess but pastoral warmth and presence; funerals and weddings and baptisms and counseling and hospital visitation and emergencies and conflict resolution and staff management; relentless pressure to write a sermon or two or three every week; and that the days of publishing articles in *NTS* and *Scottish Journal of Theology* and *Theologische Zeitschrift*—the days of being on the cutting edge of any scholarly discipline—were over.

But knowing all that, I could not resist any longer. The passion to preach and to see God shape and grow a church by the Word of God was overwhelming.

Bethlehem Baptist Church

So I was called to Bethlehem Baptist and began in June 1980. I was thirty-four years old, married with three children. The church was 110 years old, and there were three hundred older people and almost no youth. What I have done is try to preach the whole counsel of God from his written Word, with a passion for Jesus and a love for my people. I have tried to structure things so that the people are cared for in their needs and so that they learn to care for each other and reach out to the lost.

The impulses from my high school days and from Wheaton are very much alive. I am a (very slow) reader, a thinker, a feeler, a writer, a lover of poetic power, and, I hope, in all these ways, a loyal shepherd who does not forsake the sheep when the enemy comes. I have written all my sermons in manuscript form (with very few exceptions), and I try to write them with manifest rooting in the text of Scripture, with clear thinking, with strong feeling, and with imaginative surprise.

Part Two: The Scholarly Roots of Christ-Exalting Joy

It may well be asked, in what way have these thirty years of pastoral life been the work of a pastor-scholar? Let me try to answer like this—so that it has the broadest relevance and usefulness to others. At the heart of my ministry has been the conviction (which I have called *Christian Hedonism*) that *God is most glorified in us when we are most satisfied in him.*

It Is Not New

This summary statement has been the overarching theme of my life and ministry. It is the trumpet call sounding through all I say. It is not new. All I did was make it rhyme. And I'm probably not the first to do that. Jonathan Edwards said, "God is glorified not only by His glory's being seen, but by its being *rejoiced in.*"[10] That is what I am trying to say for our day: *the glory of God is magnified when we rejoice in him.*

C. S. Lewis says exactly the same thing even more clearly. In his book on the Psalms, he writes:

> The Scotch catechism says that man's chief end is "to glorify God and enjoy Him forever." But we shall then know that these are the same thing. *Fully to enjoy is to glorify.* In commanding us to glorify Him, God is inviting us to enjoy him.[11]

The implications of this for ministry are all-pervasive. I have tried to spell them out in most of my books. That is the main reason I write—to spread this conviction and this experience.

Fresh Old Language

One way the pastoral team at Bethlehem has tried to keep this issue central in all our ministry has been to develop the vocabulary of *treasuring*. *Treasure* is a wonderfully helpful word because it is both a noun and a verb in English—as it is in Greek (*thesaurus* and *thesaurizo*). God is infinitely valuable as the greatest treasure of the universe. If you find the kingdom of God, Jesus says, it is like finding a treasure hidden in a field (Matt. 13:44). Our calling in life is to manifest the greatness of the value of that treasure. The way we do it is by *treasuring* the Treasure above all things. Jesus said, "*In his joy* he goes and sells all that he has and buys that field" (Matt. 13:44). This joy—as we lose what the world has to have—is the baffling way of life that would make the world ask, "Where's your hope?" (see 1 Pet. 3:15).

In other words, at the heart of *magnifying* God's worth is *feeling* God's worth. Treasuring the Treasure. Enjoying the glory. Admiring the greatness. Savoring the feast. All this is the necessary precursor to behavior that glorifies God. If you try to do deeds "for the glory of God" without *treasuring* the glory of God in your heart, it is a sham. The word *hypocrisy* was created precisely for the effort to say with deeds what we do not feel in our hearts.

Nonchipper, Blood-Earnest Joy

So my ministry is driven by the effort to abolish this hypocrisy. It focuses on the glory of God and the joy of the soul. And, of course, this joy cries a lot. There is nothing chipper about it. We do not live in a chipper world, and Jesus did not accomplish a chipper salvation in a chipper way. Everything is blood-earnest, even our play. Even our belly laughter that lasts so long it makes our eyes red. Paul's phrase "sorrowful, yet always rejoicing" (2 Cor. 6:10) is the banner that flies over the house of Christian hedonism.

The flavor of our God-glorifying joy in God tastes like this:

> All gracious affections that are a sweet [aroma] to Christ, and that fill the soul of a Christian with a heavenly sweetness and fragrancy, are brokenhearted affections. A truly Christian love, either to God or men, is a humble brokenhearted love. The desires of the saints, however earnest, are humble desires: their hope is a humble hope; and *their joy, even when it is unspeakable, and full of glory, is a humble brokenhearted joy*, and leaves the Christian more poor in spirit, and more like a little child, and more disposed to a universal lowliness of behavior.[12]

So for thirty years I have tried, with much imperfection and manifold failures, to live up to my own message, to penetrate the heart and awaken the kind of affections for God that would accord with his glory, and create lives that would make him look great. This has been based on the conviction that *God is most glorified in us when we are most satisfied in him.*

The Downside of the Scholarly Bent

Now, how does this relate to the pastor as scholar? On the one hand, its first effect is to protect the church from the dangers of a scholarly bent. Many pastors, especially those who love the glorious vision of God's being and beauty and plan of salvation, have a scholarly bent that threatens to over-intellectualize the Christian faith, which means they turn it mainly into a system to be thought about rather than a way of life to be felt and lived. Of course, it *is* a system as well as a life. But the danger is that the whole thing can be made to feel academic rather than heart-wrenchingly real. That's what Christian hedonism helps us to avoid.

Where the faith is over-intellectualized, many ordinary, authentic saints can smell the error. Rightly, they start drifting away, but sadly, often into the worst extremes of emotionalism. But if Christian hedonism is alive—that is, if true joy in God is alive for the glory of God—I have found that many starving saints make their way home to a place where head and heart are more in balance, and the reality and power of the Holy Spirit are craved and cherished.

But this also assumes something about the head as well as the heart. If head and heart are to be in biblical balance, what is the function of the head in Christian hedonism? This is where the pastor as scholar begins to take on relevance.

The Link between Christ-Exalting Joy and
Scholarly Effort

The question here is how the life of the mind relates to treasuring Christ—how thinking relates to joy in God. I would state it like this: *Right thinking about God exists to serve right feelings for God.* Logic exists for the sake of love. Reasoning exists for the sake of rejoicing. Doctrine exists for the sake of delight. Reflection about God exists for the sake of affection for God. The head is meant to serve the heart.

So knowing truth is the proper means to admiring truth. Both thinking and feeling are indispensable. But they are not both ultimate. Thinking exists to serve admiring. Thinking is meant to serve worship and delight and satisfaction in God.

The Devil himself has many right thoughts about God. My guess is that the Devil, on some doctrines, is more orthodox than us—more correct than we are. But none of these doctrines, in the mind of the Devil, gives rise to any love for God, any worship of God, any delight in God. The Devil believes that Jesus died for sinners. The Devil believes that Jesus rose from the dead. The Devil believes that Jesus is coming back. And the Devil hates him! So knowing right things about Jesus doesn't automatically produce right affections. But knowing those right things about Christ is essential for having right affections for God.

What I am getting at is that Christ-exalting joy depends on right thinking about God. If God is going to be glorified in our being satisfied in him, then our satisfaction in him must be based on truth. And truth is what we find by the right use of the mind—by scholarly effort.

Gladness without Grounds Does Not Glorify

Let me try to illustrate why it is that a well-founded, well-reasoned delight honors Jesus. Suppose that you are walking down a street and a total stranger comes up to you and gives you a bag with $10,000 in it and asks you to deposit that money in his bank account and gives you his bank account number and his Social Security number and all his passwords. And suppose you don't know this man at all.

You ask him, "Who are you and why are you trusting me with $10,000 in cash to deposit in your bank account? Why don't you think I will steal it?"

And he says, "I don't have any reason at all for trusting you. I just feel this warm feeling in my heart that you are a trustworthy person."

Now the question is, do you feel honored by that warm feeling in his heart? No. You don't feel honored. He's crazy! He's irrational! He has no reason to trust you. He doesn't know you. He is not using his mind. He is not being a good "scholar." We are not honored by good, deep feelings toward us if they don't have any basis.

But, suppose when you ask him, "Why are you trusting me?" he says, "You don't know me, but I have been watching you at work for over a year, learning about your character. I know you very well, and I have found you to be a reliable person. Therefore, I have a joyful confidence that you will not steal my money. You are a person of character, and I have reasons for believing that."

Now, do you feel honored by the joyful feeling in that man's heart? Yes, you do. Because his emotions toward you are well-grounded. These joyful feelings of confidence and trust have reasons. They are an honor to you. They glorify you. The stranger has used his mind well—he has been a good "scholar"—and that rational effort has produced a joy in your character and trust in your reliability. This joy honors you. You are *glorified*, so to speak, in his being satisfied in you.

So, when I say that *God is most glorified in us when we are most satisfied in him*, I am referring to a well-grounded satisfaction. I see real things in Jesus and in God the Father; I see real reasons for being satisfied in him. And therefore my emotions are truly an honor to him because they are based on real reasons.

So the mind is supposed to be engaged in seeing reality for what it is, and awakening the heart to love God for all that he is. If I were to claim the role of pastor-scholar, this is what I would mean by it. Think rightly and deeply about the Word and the world with a view to seeing the greatness of God and his works (especially the work of Christ) so that the affections of our hearts might rest on a true foundation and God might be honored by how we feel toward him and by the behaviors that flow from this heart.

The Biblical Basis for the Scholarly Service of Joy

What I would like to do in the rest of this chapter is show from the Scriptures that God's purpose for right thinking (scholarship) is to awaken and sustain satisfaction in God that glorifies him. There are at least nine pointers in Scripture to this conviction.

1) Zeal according to Knowledge

Consider the first two verses of Romans 10: "Brothers, my heart's desire and prayer to God for them is that they may be saved. For I bear them witness that they have a zeal for God, but not according to knowledge." Here is a group of people that have a zeal for God, and it is doing them no good at all! They're not even saved! We know that they're not saved, because in verse 1 the apostle Paul is praying for their salvation.

So clearly, the problem is, according to verse 2, that their zeal does not accord with knowledge. So even though Christian hedonism puts a huge weight on zeal (passion) for God, now we can see how worthless that zeal is if it's not based on true knowledge. So the use of the mind to come to true knowledge is necessary so that our satisfaction in God will be an honor to him.

2) Understanding in and through Thinking

Next consider 2 Timothy 2:7. Paul says to his young disciple Timothy, "Think over what I say, for the Lord will give you understanding in everything." Understanding is a gift of God. There it is in the second half of verse 7: "The Lord will *give* you understanding in everything." Many people believe that. And they think that the understanding will be given to them without thinking. But that's the opposite of what Paul says!

Did you notice the word "for" at the beginning of the second half of the verse? " . . . *for* the Lord will give you understanding." In other words, *because* God gives understanding, *therefore* think over what Paul says! Don't say, "Because God gives understanding, I don't need to think." And don't say, "Because I'm thinking, God doesn't need to give it to me; I can get it on my own." It's *both-and*, not *either-or*.

Think over what the apostle says *because* in and through your thinking, God gives understanding. So when I am preparing a sermon, I open my Bible, or I turn on my computer Bible program, and I begin to think about the words, conjunctions, and phrases and the order of the propositions.

Every few minutes, I pause and I say, *Oh God, open my eyes, grant me light! Grant me to see what is really here! I know that I am dependent on the Holy Spirit to see the truth that is really here.* But that does not stop me from thinking! Because Paul says, "Think over what I say." Thinking hard about biblical truth is the means through which the Holy Spirit opens us to the truth.

3) Life Given through Reasoning

Now we turn to Acts 17. The apostle Paul repeatedly entered into the synagogue in order to persuade Jews to become Christians. Now, how did he do that? Acts 17:2–3 says, "Paul went in, as was his custom, and on three Sabbath days he reasoned with them from the Scriptures, explaining and proving that it was necessary for the Christ to suffer and to rise from the dead, and saying, 'This Jesus, whom I proclaim to you, is the Christ.'"

Paul knows that these unbelievers are blind and deaf

and dead in their trespasses and sins. So you might wonder, well, if all these people are blind and deaf and dead, why is he arguing with them? So the question is, if Paul believes that these unbelievers are blind—spiritually blind—and deaf and dead, why would he even talk to them?

The answer is that God has ordained to use means to give life. He has designed that life would be given, and truth would be imparted, through Paul's reasoning. Paul knows that, according to 1 Peter 1:23, we are born again through the message of God in the gospel. And so the new birth is a supernatural Holy-Spirit–caused miracle. But God does it through reasoning over the gospel.

Do you recall what Luke said about how Lydia, in Acts 16, was saved? Paul finds a group of women beside a river, and he shares the gospel with them. He reasons with them from his mind and his mouth. And Lydia is listening, with her mind, to a rational presentation of the gospel. And Luke says, "The Lord opened her heart to pay attention to what was said." So we must have both—*both* Paul's mind imparting the gospel in understandable words to Lydia's mind *and* the Holy Spirit opening Lydia's heart to receive it. There would be no joy or hope that glorifies Jesus if there were no work of the mind in Paul and Lydia.

4) Jesus Assuming Logic

We go now to Luke 12. My point here is that Jesus assumes that human beings use logic, and he holds them accountable to use their logic well. Sometimes I have been told that Aristotelian-like logic is Western and Greek, not Hebraic or biblical, and therefore doesn't belong in the presentation of the gospel.

Let me explain briefly what I mean by Aristotelian-like logic. We all know what a syllogism is. Premise number one: *All men are mortal*. Premise number two: *Plato is a man*. Conclusion: *Plato is mortal*. That's a syllogism. Aristotle is famous for noting this. And, I believe, it came from God.

Now, you have to decide: does God hold you accountable to think clearly like that? Would God be pleased if you used a syllogism like this: *Cows have four legs. My dog has four legs. Therefore, my dog is a cow*. I don't think God would be pleased if you really thought that way. That's bad logic. It's the sort of logic thugs use to put you in a dictator's jail, and it gives you no recourse to "reason." Might makes right when logic is relativized.

Now, of course, you should care little about my opinion about logic. But you should care a lot about what Jesus thinks about logic. So listen carefully to Luke 12:54–57:

> [Jesus] . . . said to the crowds, "When you see a cloud rising in the west, you say at once, 'A shower is coming.' And so it happens. And when you see the south wind blowing, you say, 'There will be scorching heat,' and it happens. You hypocrites! You know how to interpret the appearance of earth and sky, but why do you not know how to interpret the present time? And why do you not judge [that is, use your minds] for yourselves what is right?"

Notice the syllogism implied in verse 55. Jesus is saying to these people, you are really good at using your minds when it comes to matters like weather. So here's the syllogism. Premise number one: *It always gets hot when a south wind blows*. Premise number two: *A south wind is blowing*. Conclusion: *It will be hot today*. Now that is Aristotelian-like logic, which I believe, rightly construed, is straight out of the mind of God and confirmed by the example of Jesus and Jesus's holding these people accountable to use it well.

What do you think he means in verse 57? "Why do you not judge for yourselves what is right?" Your minds are so effective when they're dealing in natural things! But when your minds are applied to spiritual things, you don't think clearly at all! It would be like contemporary secular people being able to do amazing scientific things—create medicines, create computers, put people in space. Secular man, without the gospel, uses his mind in amazing ways. I think Jesus would say to a university-educated secular person, "Why do you not use your brilliant mind to understand and know me?" That's what the mind is for—to know the truth and to awaken affections for God that correspond to his greatness.

5) A Use of the Mind That Jesus Hates

Now consider Matthew 21:23–27. There is a use of the mind that Jesus hates. And I want you to ask as we look at this paragraph, *What are these people doing with their minds that Jesus abominates?*

> And when he entered the temple, the chief priests and the elders of the people came up to him as he was teaching, and said, "By what authority are you doing

these things, and who gave you this authority?" Jesus answered them, "I also will ask you one question, and if you tell me the answer, then I also will tell you by what authority I do these things. The baptism of John, from where did it come? From heaven or from man?" And they discussed it among themselves, saying, "If we say, 'From heaven,' he will say to us, 'Why then did you not believe him?' But if we say, 'From man,' we are afraid of the crowd, for they all hold that John was a prophet." So they answered Jesus, "We do not know." And he said to them, "Neither will I tell you by what authority I do these things."

What are they doing with their minds? These are very bright people. And they say, "Well, if we give him this answer, we're trapped because we didn't believe. But if we give him the other answer, we're also trapped because the people are going to be angry with us. So how can we get out of the trap? Let's use our minds to get out of the trap. Here's a good way to get out of the trap. We will say, *We don't know.*"

Frankly, that behavior makes me angry. We are surrounded in America by people like that. Instead of using their minds to come to strong convictions and let the chips fall where they will and suffer for what's true, they are repeatedly angling to get out of traps. Don't be like this, if for no other reason than because it is bad scholarship! If your mind, in studying the truth, leads you to a conviction that will get you into trouble, believe it! Speak it! There are so many pastors who conceal their convictions from their people because they are afraid of conflict.

Here's one verse that is the exact opposite of the way

these people use their minds—2 Corinthians 4:2: "But we have renounced disgraceful, underhanded ways. We refuse to practice cunning or to tamper with God's word, but by the open statement of the truth we would commend ourselves to everyone's conscience in the sight of God." That is a beautiful description of a godly pastor. I want to be that kind of preacher. I want to stand before God on the last day and say, I tried to be faithful and let people think of me what they wanted to think. I don't want to be the kind of pastor who's always watching what people are going to say and then governing what comes out of his mouth by what the people are going to say.

So good scholarship—good use of the mind in seeking and finding truth—stands in the service of honest, courageous ministry. And the goal of that ministry, whether it succeeds or not, is to put people's souls on a solid footing. The aim is that great affections for God would be awakened by clearly seen and courageously spoken truth.

6) Paul's Rhetorical Question

Thirteen times in Paul's letters, he uses the rhetorical question, "Do you not know?" Let me just give you a few examples. Do you not know that your body is the temple of the Holy Spirit? (1 Cor. 6:19). Do you not know that we will judge angels? (1 Cor. 6:2). Do you not know that when you lie with a prostitute, you become one body with her? (1 Cor. 6:15). Do you not know that a little leaven leavens the whole lump? (1 Cor. 5:6). Do you not know that the unrighteous will not inherit the kingdom? (1 Cor. 6:9). Do you not know that your bodies are members of Christ? (1 Cor. 6:15).

Thirteen times Paul uses that question. What is he thinking when he does that? He's thinking, "If you *knew*, you would be acting differently! If you *knew* these things, your hearts would be different!" He is writing his letters to help them have the kind of *knowledge* that will change their lives. This is the way we transform our churches. We don't manipulate them and coerce them into trying to act certain ways. We seek to awaken affections in the heart, for out of the heart the mouth speaks and the body acts.

My wife and I visited a church in North Carolina once while we were on vacation. My wife, who is very tolerant, left the church saying, "I don't think we will ever go back there." That's pretty verbal for her. The preacher had spent his whole sermon hammering on his people to come to the midweek meetings on Wednesday nights! And hammering on them to give money!

We sat there thinking, *This isn't working*. We just wanted to go away. And the people *were* going away. And the only thing he knew to do to help them not go away was to tell them, *Don't go away! Going away is not right!* Which is not what Paul did. Paul said, "*Don't you know* that it is more blessed to give than to receive? I want you to know the joy of giving. I love you. I want you to know the blessing."

Don't try to manipulate people. Don't try to coerce people and make them do things. It has to come from inside, from their hearts. And that means they need knowledge that awakens love. People's affections are changed by what they know. Knowledge itself is, of course, not sufficient, as we have seen (the Devil has plenty). But it is necessary. The Holy Spirit uses it to awaken new desires and new wonders and joys. That is how God is exalted in changed behaviors.

7) Pastors Able to Teach

The Bible tells us in Ephesians 4:11 that Jesus has given to his church pastors and teachers. And it tells us that these pastors and teachers should be "able to teach" (1 Tim. 3:2). They should be good teachers. So all of us pastors should be thinking, God is giving me as a gift to my church. And he is telling me, *The way you will be a gift to your church is if you are an effective teacher*.

I think that implies that ordinary folks in the pew need help understanding their Bible. If the sheep did not need help understanding their Bibles, God would not have given shepherds who had to be apt to teach. The shepherds would just read the Bible on Sunday morning, and the people would see and feel all they need to. No teaching or preaching required. But that's not how Jesus set it up.

So the pastor's job is to look at the Bible and work hard to understand what's in it, and then work hard to make it understandable and attractive and compelling to our people. The story in Luke 24:32 should ignite in every pastor a passion for Bible exposition that captures the mind of his people and makes their hearts burn. The men on the Emmaus road said, "Did not our hearts burn within us while he talked to us on the road, *while he opened to us the Scriptures*?" A few months ago when I read that, I wrote in my journal, "O God, make me that kind of teacher. I want the hearts of my people to burn as I open to them the Scriptures."

That's what thinking and understanding and teaching (scholarship) are for: burning hearts for God.

8) Mental Effort Needed for the Whole Council of God

There is a phrase in Acts 20:27 that is very important in this regard. Paul says, speaking to the elders of Ephesus, "I did not shrink from declaring to you the whole counsel of God." Now, what is this "whole counsel of God"? We don't have the space here to work out all of that, but one implication is clear: in order to give to our people the whole counsel of God, it takes tremendous mental effort to find it in the Bible.

In one sense, the Bible itself is the whole counsel of God. But that's not what Paul meant here. This is too big. He didn't just read the whole Bible to them. He taught them from the Bible (Acts 19:9). There must be a faithful way to sum this up in what's called a coherent and unified whole counsel of God. And my point is, it takes mental work to find what that is and to work it out in understandable, sharable ways.

We don't read through our Bibles once or twice or ten times and suddenly know the whole counsel of God. We have to ask hard questions about how the different parts of revelation fit together. That's called "scholarship." It doesn't have to be in school. It just has to be careful and honest and observant and synthesizing and constructive. It's head work. And it's meant to serve the heart of our people.

I think this is why in 2 Timothy 2:15 Paul calls the expositor "a *worker* who has no need to be ashamed, rightly handling the word of truth." A "worker." It takes hard mental *work* to rightly handle the Word of God. Don't let anybody ever tell you that hard mental work is unspiritual. We are using our minds to understand God's Word, and we are depending in prayer upon the Holy Spirit to guide our minds.

9) The Hard Mental Work of Book Reading

The Bible is a book. Jesus came in the flesh and was called the Word of God. He taught many things, and he did many things. He died for sins, and he rose again. He founded the church and poured out the Holy Spirit. All that foundational speaking and doing is preserved in a book. My ninth point is simply this: reading a substantial book well is hard mental work.

You learned your native language when you were very young—before you were five years old. You didn't know you were working when you did it. And so most of us assume that reading just comes naturally. But there is more than one kind of reading. One kind is passive and involves very little aggressive effort to understand. We just take what comes and let it happen to us.

But there is another kind of reading that is very active, and digs down into the author's mind, and wants to understand everything it sees. It may sound strange to say it, but one of the most scholarly things I ever learned was that many parts of the Bible (like Paul's letters and Jesus's sermons) are less like strings of pearls and more like chains of steel. That is, the authors don't just give a sequence of spiritual gems; they forge a chain of logical argumentation. Their statements hang together. They are linked. One connects to another, and those two connect to another, and those three to another, and so on as the unbreakable argument of glorious truth extends through a passage. And, when the Holy Spirit enlightens our minds, this chain of argumentation is on fire.

Rigorous reading—scholarly reading—traces these lines of argumentation. Consider Romans 1:15–21. I have reproduced this passage with each proposition on a separate line along with the verse numbers to the left. Each proposition begins with a logical connecter ("for," "that is," "as," "because," "ever since"), which appears in bold type. These small words are among the most important in the Bible. They tell us how the statements are related to each other.

For example, verse 16b gives us the *reason* that Paul is not ashamed of the gospel (16a)—namely, because it is the power of God for salvation. Verse 19a gives us the reason that God's wrath is justly revealed against *all* ungodliness everywhere in the world, even among peoples who have not access to the Bible (v. 18)—namely, because what they need to know to be held accountable is plain to them. And verses 19b–20b tell us why it is plain to them—namely, because God has revealed it in the things he made.

15 I am eager to preach the gospel to you also who are in Rome.

16 **For** I am not ashamed of the gospel,

16b **for** it is the power of God for salvation to everyone who believes,

16c **[that is]** to the Jew first and also to the Greek.

17a **For** in it the righteousness of God is revealed from faith for faith,

17b **as** it is written, "The righteous shall live by faith."

18 **For** the wrath of God is revealed from heaven against all ungodliness and unrighteousness of men, who by their unrighteousness suppress the truth.

19a **For** what can be known about God is plain to them,

19b **because** God has shown it to them.

20a **For** his invisible attributes, namely, his eternal power and divine nature, have been clearly perceived,

20b **ever since** the creation of the world, in the things that have been made.

20c **So** they are without excuse.

21a **For although** they knew God,

21b they did not honor him as God or give thanks to him,

21c **but** they became futile in their thinking,

21d **and** their foolish hearts were darkened.

On and on the chain of argumentation grows. Words become statements, and statements are linked to form larger units. And these larger units are linked to build the whole book of Romans. The point here is simply this: since much of the Bible is written this way, pastors are called to trace these arguments with active, careful, rigorous reading, and explain statements and the connections and the larger units to their people, and then apply them to their lives. This kind of reading is exceedingly demanding, and it is a large part of what I would call "scholarship."

All this is involved in the fact that God revealed himself to the church through the centuries in a book. He did not have to give the church a book. He could have done it another way. He could have just given daily dreams to his people. He could have caused dramatizations to appear in the sky. He could have communicated to a select few with secret knowledge and made them memorize everything and pass it on to another select few in each generation. He could have communicated to us any way he wanted to. And he did it in a book.

This is one reason that everywhere the Christian church has spread, there have been not only churches and hospitals, but also schools—places of rudimentary and then advanced scholarship. It's because we're dependent on a book. Since our faith is rooted in the understanding of a book, we want people to learn how to read, and then to have the Bible in their language, and to learn how to think carefully and doctrinally about the book.

So the very existence of the Bible as a book signals that the pastor is called to read carefully and accurately and thoroughly and honestly. That is, he is called to be a "scholar."

Summing Up

One way to make sense of this chapter is to say that its two parts reflect the two things that were happening to me in the first thirty-four years of my life—on the way to the pastorate. That story is the story of the emergence of a pastor with a desperate desire for joy in God and a rational bent that makes him less useful in many settings, and more useful in a few. Then the second half of the chapter is the fleshing out of those two traits—joy and thinking.

It seems to me, from my very biased and finite perspective, that what God was doing in my whole life was preparing me to see, and think about, and savor, and proclaim the truth that *God is most glorified in us when we are most satisfied in him.* The first half of the chapter describes the emergence of a sinful soul who thinks and feels deeply and loves to speak and write about it. The second half of the chapter describes how the thinking serves the feeling in the ministry of the Word.

If I am scholarly, it is not in any sense because I try to stay on the cutting edge in the discipline of biblical and theological studies. I am far too limited for that. What "scholarly" would mean for me is that the greatest object of knowledge is God and that he has revealed himself authoritatively in a book; and that I should work with all my might and all my heart and all my soul and all my mind to know and enjoy him and to make him known for the joy of others.

Surely this is the goal of every pastor.

The Scholar as Pastor

CHAPTER TWO

The Scholar as Pastor: Lessons from the Church and the Academy

D. A. Carson

To prove how wonderfully I can mangle fundamental homiletical principles, I shall proceed with an introduction divided into five parts, followed by a main body with an apostolic number of points. For my purposes, I will not count Paul, so there are only twelve points. But first:

Part One: Introduction

1) *The Pastor as Scholar and the Scholar as Pastor*—to begin by criticizing the title is usually a cheap shot, but in this case, there is an ambiguity that needs to be exposed. In England, where I lived for nine years, this title might be thought presumptuous. Over there, *scholar* is a not a word by which you would usually define yourself; rather, it is a word that someone else might use of you, if you are exceptionally gifted in your field. In other words, over there *scholar* tends to be a measure of one's competence; the word for the corresponding role is probably *academic*. So could the title of this book morph easily into *The Pastor as Academic and the Academic as Pastor*?

Now you can see that there is an issue at stake beyond the word preferred by one side or the other of the Big Pond. An "academic" is normally thought of as someone with a post in an academic institution. In that sense, an academic is not a pastor, unless a bi-vocational, part-time pastor; conversely, a full-time, vocational pastor is not an academic, except perhaps in the sense of offering some part-time courses in an academic setting.

Immediately the discussion becomes still more complicated when we recall how some larger churches, not least Bethlehem Baptist Church where John Piper serves, begin their own parallel training schools, in this case The Bethlehem Institute, currently morphing into Bethlehem College and Seminary. Is this department of Bethlehem Baptist Church rightly called an academic institution? If so, when we speak of academic pastors or pastoral academics, must there be some kind of institutional affiliation for the categories to take on meaning?

Lest we wallow in a semantic quagmire, we abandon *academic* and retreat quickly to the word *scholar* and acknowledge that, even here in North America, it can refer to either an academic role or a relatively advanced degree of competence in a particular field. The title may sound self-promoting to British ears, but the lovely ambiguity means that when we talk about, say, a pastor-scholar, we are not *reduced* to talking about institutional affiliations and the like (though we may include such reflections), but about pastoral work in the framework of rather more advanced technical competence than is customarily the case—a competence that may or may not have an institutional outlet.

He Gives Different Gifts

2) This is the time, I think, to recognize that God assigns hugely different gifts, so that one of the things this book must *not* do is give the impression that there is only one legitimate path to working out pastoral and scholarly vocations. Arnold Dallimore was a Baptist pastor who studied theological training with my dad. His only degree, his terminal degree, was a bachelor of theology. For forty years he served one church in the small Ontario town of Cottam. Nevertheless, he also set himself the task of mastering material on George Whitefield. It became a hobby, a summer challenge, a life goal. He traveled frequently to England, ransacked archives, found material that no one had ever used before and wrote his magnificent two-volume biography of Whitefield.[1] Few books make me weep, but on occasion that biography did. For all its technical competence and heavy documentation, it made me pray, more than once, *Oh, God, do it again!*

But no one insists that every pastor has the intellectual gift and long-term stamina to do the research and writing that that magnificent project entailed. John Piper has advanced training from Munich. He has been known to write poetry *in German*. Few of us can claim similar research and writing skills. Tim Keller has taught in a seminary but for years has served as a pastor—but which of us does not admire his *The Reason for God*,[2] probably the most important apologetic for outsiders since C. S. Lewis penned *Mere Christianity*?[3] So are these the sorts of examples one should call to mind when one reflects on "the scholar as pastor"?

My purpose in listing these men is twofold: *first*, more significant than the formal education are the gifts of intellectual curiosity and rigor, of focus and stamina, of lonely research and writing, that some have and some do not; and *second*, although some of these gifts can be cultivated and nurtured, precisely because some have these gifts and some do not, it would make no sense to set up an arbitrary standard as if all could and should attain them. It makes no sense to pretend you are something you are not. Some scholars will never display great pastoral gifts; some pastors will never function as gifted scholars.

A Frequently Abused Text

3) We should not proceed much farther without some brief reflections on one frequently abused text that is often applied to our topic. There is an evangelical tradition that treats what Jesus calls the "greatest" or "first" commandment as authorization for all Christian intellectual endeavor. Does not Jesus himself instruct us on this matter? He says that the most important command is this: "Hear, O Israel: The Lord our God, the Lord is one. Love the Lord your God with all your heart and with all your soul and with all your *mind* and with all your strength" (Mark 12:29–30).[4] Here, surely, is a dominical mandate for evangelical scholarship.

Well, yes and no. Certainly Jesus's words lay a heavy emphasis on thought, on engaging our whole person, focusing on how we *think* as we love God—more so than our English translations always allow us to perceive. In English, to love someone with our heart (as in "I love you with all my heart") bespeaks emotion: The heart becomes the focus of emotional engagement, while the head becomes the focus of mental or cerebral engagement. But in the Bible, the "heart" is the center of our entire being, not just of our emotions. In other words, it is very close to what we mean by "mind," except that it includes emotion, will, and value system.

So to love God with all your *heart* and with all your soul and with all your *mind* and with all your strength includes a huge emphasis on what and how we *think*; the other two words—*soul* and *strength*—bespeak intensity, total engagement. Transparently, this means that using our minds and wills in a lazy, slapdash, or arrogant way is not only pathetic, but it verges on the blasphemous. And since all truth is God's truth, we are not far from the inference that all Christian intellectual endeavor offered cheerfully and wholeheartedly to God—that is, all Christian *scholarship*—lies close to the heart of our calling. Whether you are tackling the exegesis of Psalm 110 or examining the tail feathers of a pileated woodpecker, you are to offer the work to God and see such intellectual endeavor, such scholarship, as part and parcel of worship.

Yet we cannot forget that Mark 12 and Deuteronomy 6, from which Jesus draws the first commandment, do not tell us to exercise heart and soul and mind and strength in order simply to *understand* God better. The commandment is to *love* him. Indeed, in the context of Deuteronomy 6, this love is expressed in knowing and following his words, not least in passing them on to the next generation. Love for God must never degenerate into protestations of passion without thought, into sentimental twaddle. It must be shaped by thinking God's thoughts after him, and loving him precisely in and through and by means of knowing and delighting in his words—which is precisely why there is so much emphasis on mind and volition.

So just because I study the half-life of a quark, a pileated woodpecker, the consistory records of Geneva in the years after Calvin's death, the destructive influence of Richard Simon, or a Hebrew infinitive construct does not guarantee that I love God better. In fact, it may seduce me into thinking I am more holy and more pleasing to God, when all I am doing is pleasing myself: I *like* to study. After all, plenty of secularists are fine technical scholars who enjoy their work and make excellent discoveries and write great tomes, without deluding themselves into thinking that they thereby prove they love God and deserve high praise in the spiritual sphere. Nothing is quite as deceitful as an evangelical scholarly mind that thinks it is especially close to God *because* of its scholarship rather than because of Jesus.

Nevertheless, as soon as this warning has been delivered, we must immediately repudiate the pendulum swing that favors anti-intellectualism. We *are* to love God with our *hearts* or (in the biblical sense) with our *minds*. Or again, the very business of training others involves the closest use of the mind: "The things you have heard me *say* [which surely entails texts understood by mind] in the presence of many witnesses entrust to reliable people who will also be qualified to *teach* others [which certainly requires the life of the mind, though it requires more than that]" (2 Tim. 2:2).

In short: biblical warnings about how knowledge puffs up but love builds up (e.g., 1 Corinthians 8) do not condone anti-intellectualism; conversely, biblical mandates to love God with our minds do not grant scholarship an elevated status that exempts it from adoration, faith, obedience, and love. At some level, scholarship without humility and obedience is arrogant; talk of knowing and loving God without scholarship is ignorant.

Focusing on Biblical and Theological Scholarship

4) So far I have been painting with a broad brush. I have referred to a wide sweep of scholarly disciplines, from ornithology to European history to biblical exegesis. But in the rest of this chapter, I shall focus on biblical and theological scholarship, including those disciplines, such as church history and historical theology, that may most directly strengthen the pastor's grasp. Institutionally, therefore, I am not thinking primarily about universities, Christian and otherwise, but about seminaries and similar institutions; topically, I am not now focusing on every discipline but on those most tightly related to faithful pastoral ministry. The reason, of course, is that I am supposed to be talking about the scholar as pastor, and I doubt if the Henry Center, when it issued its invitation, was thinking about how theoretical physicists might be faithful bi-vocational pastors.

This is the place where I should probably offer one further clarification. In this address, I am not unpacking all the disciplines and habits that go into how a Christian scholar ought to function *as a scholar*. That is a hugely important topic, but it is not the one I am addressing here. I am thinking, instead, of the biblical-theological scholar *as pastor*.

My Own Pilgrimage

5) Probably I should say a word about my own pilgrimage. As an undergraduate, I went to Canada's McGill University and studied chemistry. My intention was to pursue a PhD in organic synthesis; my dream was to do it at Cornell. The steps the Lord took to move me toward vocational ministry were multiple. For a start, the pastor of the church I attended in Montréal approached me one spring and told me he wanted me to intern with him that summer. I told him that, owing to the significant number of college-age students in the church, he was doubtless confusing me with someone who was planning to head into ministry. As for me, I was heading for a life in chemistry. He persisted, and so did I. We had a two-hour scrap, and I won: I went to another city that summer and worked in a chemistry lab. Nevertheless, this pastor, doubtless working out of 2 Timothy 2:2, was the first person who got me to wonder about whether I *should* be thinking of vocational ministry.

Some time later I was working in a chemistry lab in Ottawa, Canada's capital. I thoroughly enjoyed the work. Nevertheless, I soon discovered that most of my colleagues in the lab could be divided into two groups. On the one side were those who hated their jobs and were hanging on until retirement saved them from it; on the other side were those for whom chemistry was god. I didn't fit into either group. Meanwhile, I was helping a young minister with his Sunday school in a fledgling work up the valley where he was trying to plant a church, and the challenges of that minor ministry began to capture more of my imagination than the chemistry. Somewhere along the line, the words of a chorus I had sung as a boy played incessantly in my mind:

> By and by when I look on his face—
> Beautiful face, thorn-shadowed face—
> By and by when I look on his face,
> I'll wish I had given him more.[5]

Of course, I knew full well that some people are called to chemistry, or to become plumbers, nurses, or garage mechanics. The old sense of *vocatio* is important: all of us, in whatever vocational calling we have, are to offer up our work gratefully and faithfully to God as a component of our adoring worship, whether we are collecting garbage or making violins. Still, in my case I could picture approaching the judgment seat of Christ and saying, "Here, God, here's my chemistry," without having given adequate thought to what else I might have offered.

And then, early that autumn, I heard a missionary by the name of Richard Wilkerson preach on Ezekiel 22:30: "I looked for someone among them who would build up the wall and stand before me in the gap on behalf of the land so I would not have to destroy it, but I found no one." It hit me very hard. It was as if God by his Spirit was compelling me to say, "Here, please send me!"

When the Lord called me into the ministry—the potted biography does not do justice to how this was a strange and complicated time in my life—my aim was to preach, pastor, and plant churches. I had no intention of pursuing advanced degrees in biblical studies or theology. But some years later, while serving a church in the metropolitan Vancouver area, I was asked to fill in from time to time at a small, local Baptist college. I was merely covering for a few faculty members when they were ill or providing input as a local pastor.

When a normal vacancy turned up on their faculty, however, the dean asked me to apply. I declined. I was a pastor and enjoying the ministry; this was the front line. Nevertheless, the invitation served to make me wonder if I should get more training while I was still young and single. Our church was growing; we had bought property next door, a precursor to expansion. I realized that if I stayed another year, I would have to stay for five because, all things considered, it is the part of prudential wisdom not to leave in the middle of major expansion.

To cut a long story short, I resigned and went to Cambridge University, where I had three very happy years working on a PhD and speaking on occasion. Afterward, I looked at my records and discovered I had preached or taught the Bible an average of 2.6 times a week for the years I was there, so at no point had I been entirely disengaged from pastoral ministry, even though I was a full-time research student. By the end of that time, I was married, and my wife and I returned to Vancouver where I took up a post at that same college, while my wife and I helped to plant another church.

Some years later, in another providential twist, I found myself at Trinity Evangelical Divinity School (TEDS). I had not sought the post, but in God's providence it came to me, and I have served there for more than thirty years. So far, the most serious temptations I have had to leave my present post and go elsewhere have not been to join another faculty, whether at a seminary or a department in a university (though I have had both), but to return to full-time pastoral ministry. I was very close to heading in that direction some years ago when Carl F. H. Henry and Kenneth S. Kantzer descended on me with prophetic fervor and told me in rather intense ways that if I left TEDS at that point, I would be defying what God had called me to do.

By saying this, they were *not*—emphatically *not*— relegating pastoral ministry to some second tier. I have seen both of those men steer PhD graduates into pastoral ministry. Both were churchmen; they had the highest regard for the priority of pastoral ministry. Perhaps they thought I was not very qualified for it and thought I would be better at a quartermaster's job than on the frontline. But the reason they gave me was that they thought, at the time, that some of the material I was writing met certain needs, and they did not want me to take a post that was likely to reduce my output. To be perfectly frank, I still wrestle occasionally with whether they were right.

So much, then, for the five points of my introduction. I think I'd have preferred to devote the rest of this chapter to the theme of the pastor as scholar, but John Piper has done that more ably than I could, and, not surprisingly, I have been asked instead to address the theme of the scholar as pastor. Perhaps I should revise it to read "The Scholar as (Frustrated) Pastor." Out of the lessons I have learned, I offer a dozen.

Part Two: Lessons for the Scholar as Pastor

1) Take Steps to Avoid Becoming a Mere Quartermaster

Now, any army needs quartermasters. They are the ones who provide the supplies to the frontlines. By all means, give appropriate honor to those who devote themselves to equipping and supplying—with books, training, courses, modeling, answering questions—those who will be on the frontlines. Yet it is possible to write learned tomes on apologetics without actually defending the gospel in the current world; it is possible to write commentaries without constantly remembering that God makes himself present, he discloses himself afresh, to his people, through the Word.

If you are an academic, you need to put yourself into places where, as it were, you take your place with the frontline troops from time to time. This means engaging the outside world at a personal level, at an intellectual and cultural level; it means working and serving in the local church; it means engaging in evangelism. Avoid becoming a *mere* quartermaster.

I suppose I was at least somewhat shielded from initial temptations along these lines because I had been a pastor and was still preaching and teaching. My research area had to do with some elements of theology in John's Gospel against assorted Jewish backgrounds. My *Doktorvater* was a brilliant man who on many fronts had become convinced of what was essentially a naturalist approach to most biblical texts.

After I had been in Cambridge for several months and the initial glory of this spectacular university had faded at least a little, one Tuesday afternoon I was in my mentor's office for a supervision on the background to the notion of "new birth" in John 3. It was all very interesting, and impossibly uncontrolled, as I was finding my way around Jewish mystical texts, gnostic texts, Philonic thought, and so forth. But deep inside I was sort of grinning. For the previous weekend, I had preached in a chapel in the market town of March, and one of the village constables, a man known to be a bit of a brute, had got converted, rather dramatically. He was born again. I could not at that point read John 3 without thinking of that man. My point is that by continuing in forms of pastoral ministry, even while engaging in technical scholarship, you will not only avoid some pitfalls, but you will avoid becoming a mere quartermaster.

Perhaps more importantly, one of the effects of such discipline is that you will become a better teacher. Elsewhere I have told the story of how I came to write *The Gagging of God*.[6] It was the direct result of speaking at university "missions"—series of evangelistic addresses on university campuses—and observing firsthand the changing face of student questions. When I first began to do such work, even the atheists I met were "Christian" atheists—that is, the

God whom they disbelieved was recognizably the Christian God, which is a way of saying that the categories were still on my turf.

Eventually, however, the depth of biblical illiteracy among undergraduates changed that; more dramatically, postmodern epistemology meant that the approaches students were taking to "knowing" God and "knowing about" God and to exclusive claims for God and the like were so different from what I had been brought up with that I was doing more and more reading in these areas to make sure I could stay engaged with these new generations of students. At some point, an undergraduate young woman in the English department at the University of Cambridge asked me to address some of her friends. The meeting grew, and the evening turned out to be electric—and it suddenly dawned on me that I ought to put a book together on the subject, not only to clarify my own thinking but also to help others who were negotiating the same changes.

In short, take steps to avoid becoming a *mere* quartermaster. Unless you are actively involved in pastoral ministry in some sense or other, you will become distant from the frontlines and therefore far less useful than you might be.

2) Beware the Seduction of Applause

This can come from at least two directions. First, it can come from an academic direction. To be seduced by applause means that for you it becomes more important to be thought learned than to be learned. The respect of peers who write erudite journal articles becomes more immediately pressing than the Lord's approval. Obviously there is no grace in simply irritating academic colleagues, in confusing contending for the faith with being contentious about the faith. Yet if it becomes more important to you to be published by Oxford University Press or Cambridge University Press than to be absolutely straight with the gospel, if you shy away from some topics for no other reason than that these topics are unpopular in your guild, then you are in the gravest spiritual danger.

When I first arrived in Cambridge in the autumn of 1972, I suppose I reacted in the same way as do many postgraduate students who first arrive in the United Kingdom from the United States or Canada. Canada's oldest cities are only four or five hundred years old; I had been living in Vancouver, barely a hundred and fifty years old. There I was in Cambridge with parts of one church building, St. Benet's, going back a thousand years. Cambridge was at one time a Roman camp: they built a bridge over the river Cam; hence, "Cambridge." The university itself was then almost eight hundred years old, steeped in traditions; by contrast, my undergraduate university was founded in 1827, and that made it the oldest in the Commonwealth outside the British Isles. I was walking on stones where John Owen walked; my college, Emmanuel College, boasts a chapel designed by Sir Christopher Wren, who also designed St. Paul's Cathedral in London. The College Library—quite apart from the glories of the intoxicating treasures of the University Library— boasted the second-best Puritan collection in the world. It was easy for a young and inexperienced Canadian pastor to feel massively intimidated. It was easy to be more concerned about being accepted in this glorious environment, about not sticking my foot in it, than about being faithful.

In God's providence, he helped me steer clear of some of the worst excesses by the means of a serendipitous conversation I had some months after I first arrived. My *Doktorvater* was, like me at that time, single. He was high Anglican—so high that he belonged to an Anglican order of monks, the Society of St. Francis. He wore the monkish habit, had a rope around his middle instead of a belt, and, in addition to his faculty job in the university, presided over a local high Anglican church. He was also the head of the local chapter of the Society of St. Francis.

Because we were both single, we sometimes ate meals together, usually either at the chapter house or at the residential research library, Tyndale House, where I was then living. One evening after a meal together at Tyndale House, we retreated to my room for coffee. I inquired as to whether he would mind if I asked him about his spiritual pilgrimage, and he assured me he wouldn't.

I had become perplexed by his stance on all kinds of things. Usually Anglo-Catholics are pretty conservative on a wide range of critical issues, while being theologically akin to traditional Catholics on many points of doctrine. But by this time I had learned that my mentor, though very Catholic in his theological views—for instance, he had a very "high" view of the Mass—was just about as liberal as you could get on most critical issues. By "critical issues" I'm including not only matters of what is called "critical introduction"—

details about, say, the authorship of the Pastoral Epistles and of 2 Peter—but also matters concerning the historical Jesus and his person and work. So I asked him, in effect, "How did you get to your present stance on historical and theological matters? How do you become a liberal Anglo-Catholic? Isn't that an oxymoron, a contradiction in terms?"

He responded graciously by telling me something of his story. His father had been an Anglo-Catholic bishop. At the age of five, my *Doktorvater* had started learning Greek and Latin at his father's knee; Hebrew was added at the age of eleven. He had been sent along to a fine prep school. At the age of eighteen, instead of going to university he chose to go to an Anglo-Catholic training college because he wanted to enter ministry in the Anglo-Catholic wing of the Church of England and work with the poor. On graduation he joined the Society of St. Francis and worked with the poor in London for almost twenty years.

Toward the end of his thirties, he was sent by his order to work with students—and thus he came to Cambridge. He decided that the best way to work with students was to become one, so he enrolled in the university to study theology. For the first time, he came across liberal-critical views, and he bought into the lot, becoming more and more creative himself in this respect. By his own account, he went through a revolution in his own thinking and approach to the Bible. He did so well in his studies that the University asked him to teach, and his Order gave him permission. Here he was, fifteen years later, at the height of his intellectual powers, supervising my work. He loved university life and delighted in the teaching, research, and writing. His own academic star was still on the ascendancy.

I told him I appreciated his frankness, and I could see how he had arrived at his stance, but I couldn't quite see how he put it all together. For instance, I could see how someone who has a high view of Jesus, who believes that he truly is the God-man, might take the next step and have a very high view of the "host" in the Mass, seeing that somehow the deity of Jesus is present in the elements. That wasn't my view, but I understood how the connection might be made. But how could a theologian with a "low" view of the historical Jesus, an essentially naturalistic understanding of who Jesus is, then take a "high" view of the elements in Holy Communion?

I never get quite as enthusiastic in debate as John Piper, but in my plodding yet fairly intense way I was getting into the discussion, with several responses and inquiries back and forth, when it suddenly dawned on me that my mentor was becoming red-faced and sweaty and was beginning to stutter. He simply did not have a clue how to put this together. It was not my role to embarrass him, so I backed off. I'm sure I can be a smart-mouth in debate, but on that occasion I was not trying to score points but merely to understand. And in a flash, I knew that I would rather have, in God's grace, what I had than what he had; I'd rather have the gospel, knowledge of forgiveness of sins, and a reverence for God's Word than all the academic applause in the world. I wasn't sure the two were necessarily incompatible; but at least I was sure that if you had to choose one or the other, academic applause can't compare with Jesus.

Some years later I again witnessed, but from a slightly different angle, the danger of being seduced by academic applause. John Woodbridge and I had come to the conclusion that we ought to edit a couple of tough-minded books on the doctrine of Scripture, books that ultimately became *Scripture and Truth*[7] and *Hermeneutics, Authority, and Canon*.[8] In my recruitment of writers for this project, I approached a friend I had known since Cambridge days who was then teaching at another university, and who, I knew, shared our views on how Christians are to think about Scripture and what the long-sustained history of the doctrine is. He replied that although he wished our project well, he did not want to write on a subject like that, since he thought it would queer any chance he might have of getting a post at Oxford or Cambridge, where he could eventually do a lot more good. My response was that if he took that approach to confessional matters, it would not be long before he distanced himself not only from defending the doctrine, but from the doctrine itself. And that, I regret to tell you, is exactly what happened over the ensuing years. Beware the seduction of academic applause.

The second direction from which seductive applause may come is the conservative constituency of your friends, a narrower peer group but one that, for some people, is equally ensnaring. Scholarship is then for sale: you constantly work on things to bolster the self-identity of your group, to show it is right, to answer all who disagree with it. Some scholars are very indignant with colleagues who, in their estimation, are far too attracted by the applause of unbelieving academic peers, yet these indignant scholars remain blissfully unaware of how much they have become addicted to the applause of conservative bastions that egg them on.

On the last day, we stand or fall on the approval of one person, one master, the Lord Jesus.

3) Fight a Common Disjunction

Fight with every fiber of your being the common disjunction between "objective study" of Scripture and "devotional reading" of Scripture, between "critical reading" of the Bible and "devotional reading" of the Bible. The place where this tension first becomes a problem is usually at seminary. Students enter with the habit of reading the Bible "devotionally" (as they see it). They enjoy reading the Bible, they feel warm and reverent as they do so, they encounter God through its pages, some have memorized many verses and some chapters, and so forth. Seminary soon teaches them the rudiments of Greek and Hebrew, principles of exegesis, hermeneutical reflection, something about textual variants, distinctions grounded in different literary genres, and more. In consequence, students learn to read the Bible "critically" or "objectively" for their assignments but still want to read the Bible "devotionally" in their quiet times.

Every year a handful of students end up at the door of assorted lecturers and professors asking how to handle this tension. They find themselves trying to have their devotions, only to be harassed by intruding thoughts about textual variants. How should one keep such polarized forms of reading the Bible apart? This polarization, this disjunction, kept unchecked, may then characterize or even harass the biblical scholar for the rest of his or her life. That scholar may try to write a commentary on, say, Galatians, where at least part of the aim is to master the text, while preserving time for daily devotional reading.

My response, forcefully put, is to resist this disjunction, to eschew it, to do everything in your power to destroy it. Scripture remains Scripture, it is still the Word of God before which (as Isaiah reminds us) we are to tremble—the very words we are to revere, treasure, digest, meditate on, and hide in our hearts (minds?), whether we are reading the Bible at 5:30 AM at the start of a day, or preparing an assignment for an exegesis class at 10:00 PM. If we try to keep apart these alleged two ways of reading, then we will be irritated and troubled when our "devotions" are interrupted by a sudden stray reflection about a textual variant or the precise force of a Greek genitive; alternatively, we may be taken off guard when we are supposed to be preparing a paper or a sermon and suddenly find ourselves distracted by a glimpse of God's greatness that is supposed to be reserved for our "devotions." So when you read "devotionally," keep your mind engaged; when you read "critically" (i.e., with more diligent and focused study, deploying a panoply of "tools"), never, ever, forget whose Word this is. The aim is *never* to become a master of the Word, but to be mastered by it.

4) Never Forget People

Never forget there are people out there, people for whom Christ died. We don't have mere colleagues in our institutions—we have brothers and sisters in Christ. We don't have mere students, organic sponges whose primary function is to soak up data and then squeeze it back out again on demand. Rather, in our classrooms are blood-bought children of the living God. Many of them will become vocational ministers of the gospel, cross-cultural missionaries, evangelists. They are never mere sponges; they are creatures made in the image of God, human beings who have been born again, justified by grace, organically members of the church of the living God, the dwelling place of the Holy Spirit.

Of course, a seminary is an academic institution and an educational institution. Our job is to teach, and teach well. Yet not only should a Christian scholar in a seminary environment remember what any Christian scholar in *any* academic environment should remember—that these students have been created in the *imago Dei*—but such a scholar should also recognize the ministry potential of the students and detect all the more the enormous potential found in each classroom.

Every day former students spring to mind who once sat in my classroom and who are now serving challenging and fruitful ministries. I would love to take the time to tell you of a couple, for instance, whose names I dare not divulge, both of whom graduated from both Princeton and Trinity with a 4.0 GPA, and who are now serving in a Muslim country, working with refugees. Another couple I taught twenty years ago is currently working diligently at translating the Bible into eleven languages in Papua New Guinea.

Many hundreds of pastors serve faithfully, week in,

week out, who once sat in my classroom. Some have become pastor-theologians themselves, producing outstanding material that benefits others in turn. All of us stand on the shoulders of others—the Lord has ordained it that way (2 Tim. 2:2). Just as a good pastor will not treat the sermon as an artform that is an end in itself, but a means of extending grace in the re-revelation of the Word of God, so the seminary professor will not treat lectures, papers, quizzes, and assignments as nothing more than formal hoops through which to jump in the necessarily painful passage toward a degree, but as means of grace, wisely and rightly administered, as part of a larger mentoring and shaping designed to encourage a student to be a servant of the gospel, a herald of the Word, rightly interpreting this Word of truth, a worker who does not need to be ashamed.

Moreover, at least some of your students will be carrying enormous emotional, moral, guilt baggage. Can you so handle the Word of God and apply it to their lives that you sometimes observe spectacular transformation taking place? If not, what makes you think you are qualified to teach others?

This also means that just as a pastor must be more than a preacher, but must develop warm and trusting relationships with the people he serves, so the scholar-pastor must be more than an information-generating teacher who tests nothing more than content acquisition. I repeat, the seminary is an educational institution, and we should never downplay that mission. But because of the content we teach, because of the Lord we serve, we who teach in such institutions must also be eager for relationships with students, with mentoring, with the whole person.

Of course, there are only so many hours in a day. It is impossible for one teacher to have the same sort of mentoring relationship with each student. That is why most seminaries foster chaplaincy groups or spiritual formation groups (or whatever they might be called). The students in my group will be the first ones to be invited to our home, the first ones in my office, the ones who might come along for a Saturday hike, the ones who take priority on my prayer list, and so forth. I will get to know their spouses, and sometimes their children. An occasional student has become a prayer partner.

Whatever the diversity of relationships you develop and cherish, you must see that a scholar with pastoral concerns will be more than a dispenser of information.

Never forget, there are people out there.

5) Recognize Different Gifts

Happily recognize that God distributes different gifts among scholar-pastors, as he distributes different gifts among other groups. Some will be able to teach and write, but not preach; others will be able to teach and preach, but writing may be more of a challenge. Some will be excellent writers, but perfectionists, such that their output is small but superb; others are more slapdash but gifted popularizers; some are narrowly focused specialists, while others are scholarly jacks of all trades. Some are more personable than others.

Obviously we are wise to hone and develop the gifts God gives us, but we should not slip into the trap of thinking that all scholar-pastors must be similarly endowed. As the green-eyed monster can rear its head among pastors, so also among scholars; as pride and triumphalism can cripple pastoral ministry, so also scholarly ministry. What have you but what you received? Rejoice in the service to which God has called you, and eschew both arrogance and jealousy.

Having said that, however, I must hasten to add a few lines about the importance of listening to and learning from scholar-pastors who have preceded us or who exercise wider ministry or differently focused ministry than our own. Certain habits and priorities are worth careful emulation. On my own horizon, I happily acknowledge a sense of indebtedness to an array of scholars on whose shoulders I stand rather inadequately.

Leon Morris was in many ways a straightforward confessional New Testament scholar whose gifts were steady and wisely marshaled. He was not utterly extraordinary. Nevertheless, at certain junctures in his life, he perceived crucial needs and wrote works that were prescient, prophetic, and hugely stabilizing for the next generation. One thinks especially of his *The Apostolic Preaching of the Cross*, still worth buying and reading more than four long decades after its publication.[9] He taught a generation of students that they are not necessarily selling the scholarly pass if they hold that the Gospel of John is far more historically framed than commonly held today. He produced a handful of technical pieces that responded to temporary, influential false steps in his day. One thinks, for instance, of his little book *The New Testament and the Jewish Lectionaries*.[10]

I learned quite different lessons from Kenneth Kantzer. Kantzer's breadth of learning was extraordinary; his gift of analysis and synthesis was sometimes breathtaking. He had the potential to become one of the great Calvin scholars of the twentieth century. Yet he chose to marginalize these gifts in his life in order to build Trinity Evangelical Divinity School, which until very recent years was more the product, humanly speaking, of his gifts of vision and administration than of any other agent. Yet he remained astonishingly accessible to colleagues and students alike. He was a scholar-theologian-administrator-pastor.

It would be easy to add the names of another twenty or thirty scholar-pastors who have largely shaped me, and of course the diversity of their gifts and callings attests to the truth of the point I am making: happily recognize the diversity of gifts that God gives scholar-pastors.

Perhaps this is the place where we should recognize another aspect of diversity—diversity in reading habits. A new generation has come along that turns reflexively to the web for information and reads fewer books. I don't care whether you read books in print or digital form; I am quite happy with my Kindle reader. But for all that the web makes information gloriously accessible, it has two huge shortcomings. First, it is so democratized that it is more difficult than ever to distinguish between truth and error, between authoritative opinion and fatuous opinion, between speculation and learning. Second, it swamps us with brief information and opinion; it entices us into endless worthless discussions even on blogs that may themselves be valuable.

One of the things that thoughtful scholar-pastors will do is preserve time for reflective reading of the *best* books. You can find out what those books are by having probing conversations with a variety of scholar-pastors who are more mature than you are—but be sure you seek out the opinions of several people, not just one. Through their books, get to know some epochal thinkers reasonably well. Slow down; read, take notes, think, evaluate.

Yet having said these things—things that must be said as a kind of foil to the temptations of reading exclusively on the web—I must quickly add that in this domain of reading, there is, and there should be, quite a diversity of legitimate reading practices. Some, more focused than others and perhaps slower readers and sharper thinkers than others, want you to restrict your reading to very good books that you must read slowly. For some readers, I suspect that that is the wisest choice; for all readers, reading some books slowly and analytically is mandated. But I doubt that it is wise to suggest that every scholar should read only good books and only slowly, for once again there is a diversity of gifts and graces.

If you can develop the habit of reading different things at different speeds, you might be wise to read some books slowly, evaluatively, and often; to read some books briskly, once but comprehensively; to skim other books to see what they are saying; to dip into still other books to see if they add anything to a discussion or merely say the same old things with a minor twist here and there. All that is apart from reading some poetry, some serious literature, and even occasional pieces that have no enduring value but that everyone is reading at the moment—not because you want to spend much time there, or should spend much time there, but so as to offer penetrating firsthand comments on material that virtually every literate person in your world knows something about.

Not every scholar-pastor should attempt to do all these things, but those who have the gift, the time, and the energy to do so, and who then offer their "take" on a broad array of literature, become a great gift to those of us who read more narrowly or at more limited speed. Precisely because there is a diversity of gifts, the perspective of Roger Bacon is memorable: "Reading maketh a full man; speaking maketh a quick man; writing maketh an exact man."

What is virtually *never* justified, however, is *never* reading *anything* slowly, seriously, analytically, and evaluatively, for such reading of good material not only fills our minds with many good things, but teaches us how to think.

In short, happily recognize that God distributes different gifts among scholar-pastors.

6) Recognize What Students Learn

Recognize that students do not learn everything you teach them. They certainly do not learn everything I teach them! What *do* they learn? They learn what I am excited about; they learn what I emphasize, what I return to again and again; they learn what organizes the rest of my thought. So if I happily *presuppose* the gospel but rarely articulate it and am never excited about it, while effervescing frequently about, say, ecclesiology or textual criticism, my students may conclude that the most important thing to me is ecclesiology or textual criticism. They may pick up my *assumption* of the gospel; alternatively, they may even distance themselves from the gospel; but what they will almost certainly do is place at the center of *their* thought ecclesiology or textual criticism, thereby wittingly or unwittingly marginalizing the gospel.

Both ecclesiology and textual criticism, not to mention a plethora of other disciplines and sub-disciplines, are worthy of the most sustained study and reflection. Nevertheless, part of my obligation as a scholar-teacher, a scholar-pastor, is to show how my specialism relates to that which is fundamentally central and never to lose my passion for living and thinking and being excited about what must remain at the center. Failure in this matter means I lead my students and parishioners astray.

If I am then challenged by a colleague who says to me, "Yes, I appreciate the competence and thoroughness with which you are handling ecclesiology or textual criticism, but how does this relate to the centrality and nonnegotiability of the gospel?" I may, regrettably, respond rather defensively, "Why are you picking on me? I believe in the gospel as deeply as you do!" That may be true, but it rather misses the point. As a scholar, ecclesiology or textual criticism may be my specialism; but as a scholar-*pastor*, I must be concerned for what I am passing on to the next generation, its configuration, its balance and focus. I dare never forget that students do not learn everything I try to teach them but primarily what I am excited about.

7) Make the Main Thing the Main Thing

The principle I enunciated in the previous point needs thoughtful application in quite a number of domains. In *every* area of a biblical-theological scholar's work, it is important to keep asking what is at stake, what related issues constitute the main thing. Permit me three examples.

First, consider some of the various ways scholars teach systematic theology. Some trained in philosophical theology help students work through complex notions, such as "person," when explaining patristic Trinitarian formulations: one substance but three persons. Others trained in historical theology may construct their systematics largely out of the trail of theologians who have gone before them. Both may be effective teachers; both *may* never open their Bible from the first class period in the semester to the last. That means a "main thing" has been overlooked: students with a high view of Scripture *must* be trained in how theological formulations ought to be grounded in and derive from what Scripture says. *Otherwise, what systematicians are really teaching is that the structures of systematic theology not only do not spring from Scripture but need not spring from Scripture.* In that case, how is Scripture the "norming norm" of the discipline? In propagating one aspect of the complex discipline of systematic theology, such scholars are sacrificing what is *essential* to the discipline: self-consciously drawing the connections, *for the sake of the student*, from Scripture, through historical/philosophical/hermeneutical grids, to confessional formulation.

Second, the drumbeat of our themes may do unwitting damage, even when every point we make is right. For instance, those who teach Bible, theology, and historical theology sometimes (and rightly) point out weaknesses, aberrations, and assorted blind spots in contemporary evangelicalism. This *may* work its way out in students who become more and more critical of confessional evangelicalism, and pretty soon even of the evangel itself. They are in danger of becoming smart-mouths. Their superciliousness guarantees that they cannot minister effectively anywhere. Instead of becoming believers whose lives fruitfully foster change within the church, these students become condescending critics. Not only are they less fruitful than they might have been, but they are in great spiritual danger.

All this has occurred because their teachers have not been as careful in fostering a sense of indebtedness to those who have come before as they have been in fostering what they think of as discernment. Jesus nowhere says, "By this shall all know that you are my disciples, if you are scintillatingly critical and condescending toward evangelicals who have some things wrong." I do not mean to hint for a moment that we who teach can afford to duck the responsibility of teaching discernment. I mean only to say that even discernment must be nestled into the bigger "main thing" of love for the brothers and sisters in Christ.

Third, scholarship inevitably cares about innovation, fresh discoveries, new insights. Such strengths are not to be dismissed. But if a scholar makes that sort of pursuit his or her primary passion, it will become easy to overlook or marginalize the gospel once for all delivered to the saints;

it will be easy to stand loose with respect to what must be proclaimed in *every* culture, to the gospel of Jesus who stands athwart the tides of history and cries, "Come to *me*!" In all our legitimate concern for the innovative, what is of greater importance is the changeless—and this is what has dominant pastoral importance. Let the main thing be the main thing.

8) Pray and Work for Vision

Specifically, pray and work for vision beyond that of publishers. A well-known scholar has boasted that he has never had to submit a book manuscript to any publisher, asking if they might be interested. In *every* case—and he has written many books—publishers have approached him and asked him to write something. This happens far more often than people realize, especially once a scholar has published an initial book or two. I suppose the scholar in question takes this as a point of strength, almost a matter of self-congratulation. At one level, it is powerful attestation that what he writes will be purchased, and that is why publishers want him on their lists. But what this *also* means is that this scholar has entertained no vision for research and writing beyond what publishers have asked him to tackle. That is almost unbearably sad.

If you are a pastor-scholar, you ought to be asking yourself what might be especially helpful at the present moment, what work of scholarship is crying out to be tackled, what popularization would benefit the Lord's people. Sometimes publishers will think of such things first: their invitations coincide with your interests and priorities. Where *you* think of certain topics first, however, part of your job is to "sell" a publisher on the idea, so the material can be published or achieve prominence on a better website or the like. If you write only what others ask you to write, I fear you may be displaying a want of scholarly imagination, and, still worse, a lack of pastoral care.

9) Love the Church

Love the church because Jesus loves it. Let your students *know* you love the church; make sure that the fellow members of your church are deeply aware that you love the church, that you love them. This will work out in many different ways, but such love for the church *must* find outlets in your prayer life, your priorities, your willingness to participate (with the elders? in a small group? in teaching a class? in taking your turn on a preaching rota? in helping with the cleaning? in drafting a new constitution?).

Loving the church is not only important to balance out the rugged individualism that is often part and parcel of having grown up in America and that is sometimes in danger of neglecting both communal life and strong personal relationships with brothers and sisters in Christ, *but also to stamp our students.* If we are training a preponderance of pastors and others who will serve in the local church, it is *essential* that the faculty members truly love the church that Christ loved and for which he gave himself. Many students will learn to love what their professors truly love. So love the church.

10) Avoid Lone-Ranger Scholarship

Every scholar knows that part of the task of scholarship is bound up with long, lonely hours of disciplined study and writing. Some projects, however, are better undertaken with collaboration. No less important, if you are beginning to press into arenas of thought that are not your first area of competence, you are wise to run your work by others in the field, to solicit criticisms and suggestions. Better yet, it is often good to seek out a new generation of younger scholars and embroil them in new research and writing projects, giving them books to review, soliciting their opinions, interacting with their suggestions. Not only do you yourself benefit—it is much better to receive criticism for a work before it goes to press than in the reviews after it has been released—but you are involved in a kind of scholarly mentoring that is the fruit of essentially *pastoral* commitments.

I once knew a scholar (he has gone to his reward) who produced, among other books, a remarkable reference volume that covered vast areas. It was "remarkable" because its entries ranged from the brilliantly insightful to the mediocre, then all the way down to the painfully ignorant. The volume never did have the kind of influence its author hoped it would have. He could easily have avoided such a mixed work if he had taken the time to collaborate with other scholars who legitimately claimed overlapping areas of competence and could have saved him the embarrassment of so many mediocre and ignorant entries mingled in with the brilliant.

11) Be Interested in the Work of Others

Be at least as interested in the work of others as you are in your own. This is wise not only because you do not want to become the party bore who turns every conversation and discussion toward his or her own work—a peculiarly nasty form of narcissism—but because the commandment and example of Christ compels you to seek the other's good, to love your neighbor as yourself, to promote scholarship insofar as it is explicating and promoting the truth and not just because it is *your* scholarship. Be at least as interested in the work of others as you are in your own.

12) Take Your Work Seriously, but Not Yourself

Make sure you have some people around you who feel free to laugh at you. I have no idea how many times at dinner parties and the like my wife has enjoyed poking fun at some of my titles: *Justification and Variegated Nomism*, for instance.[11] Isn't that one a winner? Walk humbly—you have far more to be humble about than you realize. Take your work seriously, but not yourself.

Concluding Comment

I have been talking about the scholar-pastor. It would take only a little imagination to see how the kinds of virtues I have been promoting have analogues in virtually *every* sphere. Is it only the scholar, for instance, who must avoid the seduction of applause? Is it only the Christian scholar who wishes to serve pastorally who must be urged to love the church? Is it only the scholar who must constantly check to ensure that the main thing is still the main thing?

In short, most of what I have been urging has correlative application in the lives of all Christians. Because the virtues and graces that go into pastoral care are essentially *Christian* virtues and graces, the application is as broad as the number of Christians.

Conclusion
The Preacher, the Professor, and the True Pastor-Scholar

David Mathis

The post–World War II baby boom began in 1946 and brought with it John Piper and Don Carson. It was only eleven days into that year, on January 11, that Bill and Ruth Piper met their newborn American boy, and roughly eleven months later, on December 21, when Tom and Marg Carson brought their new little Canadian into the world.

Both the Carson and Piper homes were ministry homes. Bill Piper was a traveling evangelist; Tom Carson was a church planter and pastor on the difficult soil of Quebec. Both homes could be described as warm-hearted fundamentalist—the kind that have often produced strong evangelical leaders.

As Piper and Carson came of age in late 1960s and ventured beyond their native fundamentalist spheres, they did not encounter the plethora of evangelical pastor-scholars our emerging Millennial generation is discovering today. F. F. Bruce (interestingly mentioned by both Pastor Piper and Professor Carson in the previous chapters) stood as an evangelical model in the scholarly world, along with the stateside forerunners of the modern evangelical movement Carl Henry and Kenneth Kantzer, but pastor-scholars were tough to find. Harold Ockenga, seminary president and pastor of Park Street Church in Boston, may have been the closest thing in the mid-twentieth century to what we've called in this book a pastor-scholar, but there weren't many like him. So when Piper and Carson earned their doctoral degrees in the 1970s, it still appeared that they would eventually come to a fork in the road where they must decide to be *either* pastor *or* scholar.

It is interesting that Piper first took the scholar's path, soon finding a growing heart for the pulpit, while Carson began on the pastoral trail and soon cultivated his world-class mind as a scholar. Piper is the scholar turned pastor; Carson is the pastor turned scholar. In 1978, Carson took an assistant professorship at Trinity Evangelical Divinity School; in 1980, Piper went to Bethlehem Baptist Church to pastor. Both have now invested in those locales for over three decades.

But as we saw in the previous chapters, Piper's mind never fully left the academy (at least with respect to a serious engagement of the life of the mind), and Carson's heart never left the church. This once rare, now increasingly common, blending of heart and head produced two extraordinarily fruitful ministries in the last thirty years that have conspired, along with others, to wean a new generation of thoughtful and pastoral evangelical leaders ready to plant and develop the churches and institutions of the twenty-first century—a new generation of spiritual leaders increasingly uneasy about leaving behind rigorous thinking for the pastorate or abandoning a pastor's heart for the academy.

From Where Has This Impulse Come?

Why has there arisen this impulse in our day toward pastor-scholars and scholar-pastors? Why are so many in the younger generation reluctant to let the pastoral and scholarly roads diverge? Among many factors, it is worth pointing to the amazing half-century explosion of the evangelical movement in the United States that is paving a two-lane road where once stood a fork. Not only have we seen a stunning advance in evangelical publications but also a proliferation of preaching and teaching via the Internet (written, audio, and now video). Combine this with the number of models the previous generation has produced—one thinks not only of Piper and Carson, but of others like Tim Keller, Al Mohler, Mark Dever, Ligon Duncan, Gordon Hugenberger, Sam Storms, and others—and, under God, you have a recipe for the revival of a new generation of Jonathan Edwards–like pastor-scholars.

Beyond these contemporary examples come the more distantly historical examples of Athanasius and Augustine, Luther and Zwingli and Calvin, along with John Bunyan, Andrew Fuller, and the Puritans.

And beyond these stalwarts is the apostle Paul, a man with both a manifestly first-rate intellect and a heart big enough to feel "the daily pressure on me of my anxiety for all the churches" (2 Cor. 11:28).[1]

Beyond Paul is the example of the truest pastor-scholar of all, who even at age twelve gave evidence of both his scholarly mind and his pastoral heart. Like a scholar, "all who heard him were amazed at his understanding and his answers" (Luke 2:47) while he responded to his parents, like a pastor, "Did you not know that I must be in my Father's house?" (Luke 2:49). When fully grown, as a scholar, he knew the Scriptures better than any and could silence the learned Pharisees with a word; and as pastor, he called children to himself and lovingly trained his disciples through their sluggishness and chronic incompetence.

Jesus, the God-man, is the ultimate model of engaging *both* heart *and* head, not compromising either for the other. He is both "the chief Shepherd" (1 Pet. 5:4) and the one whose wisdom is greater than Solomon's (Matt. 12:42). He is not only "the great shepherd of the sheep" (Heb. 13:20) and "the Shepherd and Overseer of your souls" (1 Pet. 2:25), but also in Luke 24, "beginning with Moses and all the Prophets, he interpreted to them in all the Scriptures the things concerning himself" (Luke 24:27) and was the master professor who with his teaching, by the work of his Holy Spirit, "opened their minds to understand the Scriptures" (Luke 24:45).

This new generation of Christian leaders does well to look to Piper and Carson and Keller and the others. We may do even better, in some senses, in looking to Luther and Calvin. We do better still looking to Paul. And we do best looking to Jesus.

The Importance of the Center

The temptations are great, in the life of both the pastor-scholar and the scholar-pastor, to give greater and greater attention to the peripheral things, to the multitude of marginally important subjects. The peripheral and marginal no doubt at times do need our attention, at times even great attention. But as a Christian leader, whether pastor-scholar or scholar-pastor, the servant of the Lord comes back again and again to the old, old story that is the very heart of the faith. It is the gospel that apostle Paul says is of "first importance" (1 Cor. 15:3). It is the gospel that is "the power of God for salvation" (Rom. 1:16). It is the gospel that not only saves the lost but is "at work in you believers" (1 Thess. 2:13), the gospel that is "bearing fruit and growing" (Col. 1:6), not only worldwide but in us and in our church communities. So it is the gospel that Paul leaves with the spiritual leaders of Ephesus in his farewell address to them in Acts 20: "I commend you to God and to *the word of his grace*, which is able to build you up and to give you the inheritance among all those who are sanctified" (v. 32). It is the gospel that builds up and makes us holy.

So in charging pastors to be more serious about the life of the mind, and in challenging scholars to be more engaged with the life of the church, we conclude with this prayer, that all our thoughtful shepherding and all our pastoral scholarship may be to the great end of having the gospel message about Jesus dwell richly (Col. 3:16) both in us and in our people; that knowing Jesus would be the great end of all our pastoring and our scholarship; that we ourselves, in all our preaching, writing, studying, and counseling, would continue to see ourselves as the great beneficiaries of his great grace; that into eternity we would be followers of Jesus more and more shaped, saturated, and transformed by his person and work. To Jesus, the great pastor-scholar, be the glory. Amen.

Notes

Introduction: The Return of the Pastor-Scholar

1. Media from the evening, including both talks and a question-and-answer session, may be found at http://pastortheologian.com, the specially created website for the event.

2. These lectures were given November 10–11, 2009, at The Southeastern Baptist Theological Seminary in Wake Forest, North Carolina. They were entitled "Doing Faith: Seeking (and Showing) in Company with Christ" and can be accessed at http://thegospel coalition.org/blogs/justintaylor/2010/03/18/vanhoozer-on-redrama tizing-theology/.

3. "The Pastor as Theologian: Preaching and Doctrine," in R. Albert Mohler Jr., *He Is Not Silent: Preaching in a Postmodern World* (Chicago: Moody, 2008), 105–14.

4. David Wells, *The Courage to Be Protestant* (Grand Rapids, MI: Eerdmans, 2008), 40.

5. Douglas A. Sweeney, *Jonathan Edwards and the Ministry of the Word* (Downers Grove, IL: IVP Academic, 2009), 197–200.

6. Gerald L. Hiestand, "Pastor-Scholar To Professor-Scholar: Exploring The Theological Disconnect Between The Academy And The Local Church," *Westminster Journal of Theology* 70 (Fall 2008): 356–72.

7. Daniel L. Akin, *A Theology for the Church* (Nashville: Broadman, 2007).

Chapter 1: The Pastor as Scholar

1. F. F. Bruce, *In Retrospect: Remembrance of Things Past* (Grand Rapids, MI: Eerdmans, 1980), 306.

2. Jonathan Edwards, "Some Thoughts Concerning the Revival," in *The Works of Jonathan Edwards*, vol. 4, *The Great Awakening*, ed. C. C. Goen (New Haven, CT: Yale University Press, 1972), 387.

3. Unless otherwise indicated, Scripture quotations in this chapter are from the ESV® Bible (*The Holy Bible, English Standard Version®*), copyright © 2001 by Crossway. Used by permission. All rights reserved.

4. See Appendix 2 in John Piper, *Think: The Life of the Mind and the Love of God* (Wheaton, IL: Crossway, 2010).

5. Peter Stuhlmacher, *Vom Verstehen des Neuen Testaments: eine Hermeneutik* (p. 170), echoes Schlatter: "Wissenschaft is ertstens Sehen uns zweitens Sehen and drittens Sehen und immer und immer wieder Sehen."

6. To read the rest of Kilby's resolutions for mental health, see John Piper, *The Pleasures of God* (Sisters, OR: Multnomah, 2000), 95–96.

7. My biographical tribute to Lewis, titled "Lessons from an Inconsolable Soul: Learning from the Mind and Heart of C. S. Lewis," is available at http://www.desiringgod.org/ResourceLibrary/Biographies/4503.

8. John Piper, *"Love Your Enemies": Jesus' Love Command in the Synoptic Gospels and the Early Christian Parenesis* (Cambridge: Cambridge University Press, 1979).

9. I do want to honor my late professor Leonhard Goppelt. He was, as far as I could discern, a truly godly man with a high view of the gospel and of the Lord Jesus. He was extraordinarily courteous and solicitous of me as a foreign student. His untimely death in December 1973 was tragic, and it was because of his high esteem in the eyes of his colleagues that I was able (with the help of Georg Kretchmar) to finish my degree.

10. Jonathan Edwards, "Miscellanies," in *The Works of Jonathan Edwards*, vol. 13, ed. Thomas Schafer (New Haven, CT: Yale University Press, 1994), 495, miscellany #448.

11. C. S. Lewis, *Reflections on the Psalms* (New York: Harcourt, 1958), 97; emphasis added.

12. Jonathan Edwards, *Religious Affections*, in *The Works of Jonathan Edwards*, vol. 2, ed. John Smith (New Haven, CT: Yale University Press, 1959), 348–49.

Chapter 2: The Scholar as Pastor

1. Arnold A. Dallimore, *George Whitefield: The Life and Times of the Great Evangelist of the Eighteenth-Century Revival*, vols. 1 and 2 (Banner of Truth, 1970, 1980).

2. Timothy Keller, *The Reason for God: Belief in an Age of Skepticism* (New York: Dutton, 2008).

3. C. S. Lewis, *Mere Christianity* (repr. San Francisco: HarperOne, 2001).

4. Scripture quotations in this chapter are from the Holy Bible, Today's New International Version. TNIV®. Copyright© 2001, 2005

by International Bible Society. Used by permission of Zondervan. All rights reserved.

5. Lyrics from "I'll Wish I Had Given Him More," words and music by Grace Reese Adkins, 1948 (renewed 1976, Lillenas); online at http://hymnal.calvarybaptistsv.org/393.html.

6. D. A. Carson, *The Gagging of God: Christianity Confronts Pluralism* (Grand Rapids, MI: Zondervan, 1997).

7. D. A. Carson and John D. Woodbridge, eds. *Scripture and Truth* (Grand Rapids, MI: Baker, 1983).

8. D. A. Carson and John D. Woodbridge, eds., *Hermeneutics, Authority, and Canon* (Grand Rapids, MI: Baker, 1986).

9. Leon Morris, *The Apostolic Preaching of the Cross* (Grand Rapids, MI: Eerdmans, 1956).

10. Leon Morris, *The New Testament and the Jewish Lectionaries* (London: Tyndale Press, 1964).

11. D. A. Carson, Peter T. O'Brien, and Mark A. Seifrid, eds., *Justification and Variegated Nomism*, vols. 1 and 2 (Grand Rapids, MI: Baker, 2001, 2004).

Conclusion:
The Preacher, the Professor, and the True Pastor-Scholar

1. Scripture quotations in this chapter are from the ESV® Bible (*The Holy Bible, English Standard Version*®), copyright © 2001 by Crossway. Used by permission. All rights reserved.

General Index

Akin, Daniel, 16
Anglo-Catholics, 86–87
anti-intellectualism, 37, 76–77
Apostolic Preaching of the Cross, The (Morris), 95
Athanasius, 109
atheism, 83–84
Augustine, 14, 23, 109

Bethlehem Baptist Church, 45–46, 72, 108
Bethlehem College and Seminary, 72
Bethlehem Institute, 72
Bible, the, 64, 65; revelation of God in, 66, 67; rigor required in the reading of, 63–66; as the whole counsel of God, 62–63
Bromiley, Geoffrey, 37
Bruce, F. F., 21–22, 23, 107
Bunyan, John, 23, 109

Calvin, John, 14, 109
Cambridge University, 85
Carl F. H. Henry Center for Theological Understanding, 15

Carson, D. A., 14–15, 17, 107, 108; calling of to be a pastor, 78–82; at Cambridge University, 80, 83, 85–88; education of, 76; experience of with university "missions," 83–84; friendship of with his *Doktorvater*, 86–88; at Trinity Evangelical Divinity School (TEDS), 81
Carson, Marg, 107
Carson, Tom, 107
Christians, 106
Confessions (Augustine), 23
Courage to Be Protestant, The (Wells), 16

Dallimore, Arnold, 73
Dever, Mark, 109
Devil, the, 50, 61
discipleship, 14, 41
Duncan, Ligon, 109

Edwards, Jonathan, 14, 34, 39–40, 41, 46
Emmanuel College, 85
End for Which God Created the World, The (Edwards), 40

Essay on the Trinity (Edwards), 40

evangelicalism, 37, 101; growth of in the United States, 109

evangelism, 14

Fuller, Daniel, 38–40

fundamentalism, 37

Gagging of God, The (Carson), 83

God: fear of, 27, 29; God's distribution of gifts, 94–95; God's granting of understanding to believers, 53–54; knowing God, 84; our creation in God's image (*imago Dei*), 92; our love for God, 74–77; pursuit and revelation of Gods glory through our joy, 21, 39, 46–47, 48, 49, 50–52, 67; revelation of in the Bible, 66, 67; right thinking concerning God, 51; righteousness of, 65; sovereignty of, 40, 44; treasuring of God's glory, 47; worth and value of, 47; wrath of, 64, 65. *See also* Bible, the, as the whole counsel of God

Goppelt, Leonhard, 41, 114n9

grace, 40, 43, 88, 92, 93, 111

Grace Abounding (Bunyan), 23

Hackett, Arthur, 30–31

He Is Not Silent (Mohler), 16

hedonism, Christian, 46, 49; and zeal, 53

Henry, Carl F. H., 81, 107

Henry, Noîl, 33, 35, 37

Hermeneutics, Authority, and Canon (Carson and Woodbridge), 89

Hiestand, Gerald, 16

Hirsch, E. D., 38

Holmes, Arthur, 30

Holy Spirit, the, 49, 54, 55, 59, 61, 63, 64, 92, 110

Hugenberger, Gordon, 109

Jesus, 24, 47, 48, 50, 54, 55; "first commandment" of, 74–77; and human logic, 55–57; Jesus's hatred of those who lack the conviction of their beliefs, 57–59; knowing Jesus, 111; as a model for pastor-scholars, 109–10; presence of in the host, 88; as the Word of God, 63

Jesus and the Kingdom (Ladd), 37

Jonathan Edwards and the Ministry of the Word (Sweeney), 16

joy, biblical basis for the scholarly service of, 53; and the Bible as the whole counsel of God, 62–63; calling of pastors to be teachers, 61–62; having zeal accord with knowledge, 53; and the

importance of Pauls rhetorical questions, 59–61; Jesus's assumption of human logic, 55–57; Jesus's hatred of those lacking the conviction of their beliefs, 57–59; and life given through reasoning, 54–55; and the need for rigorous reading of the Bible, 63–66; understanding arrived at through thinking, 53–54
Justification of God, The: An Exegetical and Theological Study of Romans 9:1–23 (Piper), 44

Kantzer, Kenneth S., 81, 96, 107
Keller, Tim, 73, 109
Kilby, Clyde, 32, 34

Ladd, George, 37
Lake Avenue Congregational Church, 37
Lewis, C. S., 34–35, 46, 74
Lloyd-Jones, Martyn, 14
logic, Aristotelian, 55–56
Luther, Martin, 14, 109
Lydia, 55

Men Made New (Stott), 36
Mere Christianity (Lewis), 74
Mohler, R. Albert, Jr., 16, 109
Morris, Leon, 95

New Testament and the Jewish Lectionaries, The (Morris), 95
New Testament Theology (Ladd), 37

Ockenga, Harold John, 36, 108
Ortlund, Ray, Sr., 37
Owen, John, 85

pastor-scholars, 13–14, 71–73, 105–6; and the ability to teach, 61–62; centrality of the gospel to, 110–11; influences for a revival of pastor-scholars, 109–10; and the over-intellectualizing of Christian faith, 49. *See also* pastor-scholars, lessons for
pastor-scholars, lessons for: avoid becoming a quartermaster, 82–84; avoid lone-ranger scholarship, 104; beware the seduction of applause, 84–90; fight the common disjunction between the "objective study" of Scripture and the "devotional reading" of Scripture, 90–91; importance of stressing the "main thing" in teaching different subjects, 100–102; love the church, 103; never forget people, 91–94; pray and work for vision, 102–3; recognize different gifts in

others, 94–98; recognize what students learn, 98–99; show interest in the work of others, 105; take work seriously, 105

Paul, 25, 62, 64, 109; use of reasoning by, 54–55; use of rhetorical questions by, 59–61

Perrin, Norman, 37

Piper, Bill, 107

Piper, John, 15, 17, 66–67, 73, 82, 88, 107; at Bethel College, 42–45; at Bethlehem Baptist Church, 45–46, 72; childhood of, 26–27; disillusionment of with technical scholarship, 42; doctoral studies of at the University of Munich, 41–43; faith of in Jesus, 26, 29–30; at Fuller Seminary, 36–41; high school experiences of, 27–30; opinion on speaking about what means most to him, 22–25; as a pastor-scholar, 25–26, 108; publication of his dissertation, 43; as a romantic-rationalist, 40. *See also* Piper, John, at Wheaton College

Piper, John, at Wheaton College, 30; as the bridge to a career in ministry, 35–36; influences on his heart at, 32–33; influences on his mind at, 30–32;

influences on the synthesis of mind and heart at, 34–35

Piper, Ruth, 107

Poetry and Life (Kilby), 32–33

postmodernism, 31; postmodern epistemology, 84

reading: diversity in, 97–98; importance of in scholarship, 38–39

Reason for God, The (Keller), 72–73

Schaeffer, Francis, 31

scholars: as "academics," 71–72; tasks of, 39. *See also* pastor-scholars

scholarship, 21, 26, 39, 42, 62, 65; biblical and theological scholarship, 77–78; evangelical scholarship and Jesus's "first commandment," 74–77; and innovation, 101–2; linkage between Christ-exalting joy and scholarly effort, 49–50

Scripture and Truth (Carson and Woodbridge), 89

Simon, Richard, 76

Society of St. Francis, 86, 87

Spurgeon, C. H., 14

Storms, Sam, 109

Stott, John, 36

Sweeney, Douglas, 16

systematic theology, 100

*Theological Dictionary of the
    New Testament* (Kittle), 37
Theology for the Church, A
    (Akin), 16
Trinity, the, patristic formula-
    tions of, 100
Trinity Evangelical Divinity
    School (TEDS), 96, 108

Validity in Interpretation
    (Hirsch), 38
Vanhoozer, Kevin J., 16

Wells, David, 16
Welsh, Evan, 35
Wessel, Walt, 43
*Westminster Journal of Theol-
    ogy*, 16
Whitefield, George, 73
Wilkerson, Richard, 79
Woodbridge, John, 89
Wren, Christopher, 85

Zwingli, Ulrich, 109

Scripture Index

Deuteronomy
6   75

Psalms
110   75

Song of Solomon
8:4   33

Ezekiel
22:30   79

Matthew
12:42   110
13:44   47
21:23–27   57

Mark
12   75
12:29–30   74

Luke
2:47   109
2:49   110
12   55
12:54–57   56
12:55   56
12:57   57
24   110

24:27   110
24:32   61
24:45   110

John
3   83
5:44   24

Acts
16   55
17:2–3   54
19:9   62
20   111
20:27   62
20:32   111

Romans
1:15   65
1:15–21   64
1:16   65, 111
1:16a   64
1:16b   64, 65
1:16c   65
1:17a   65
1:17b   65
1:18   64, 65
1:19a   64, 65
1:19b   65
1:19b–20b   64
1:20a   65

1:20b	65
1:20c	65
1:21a	65
1:21b	65
1:21c	65
1:21d	65
10:1	53
10:2	53

1 Corinthians

5:6	59
6:2	59
6:9	59
6:15	59, 60
6:19	59
8	77
15:3	111

2 Corinthians

1:8–9	25
4:2	59
6:10	48
11:28	109

Ephesians

1:11	40
4:11	61

Philippians

1:12–13	25
2:3	24

Colossians

1:6	111
2:1–2	25
3:16	111

1 Thessalonians

2:13	111

1 Timothy

3:2	61

2 Timothy

2:2	77, 78, 93
2:7	53
2:15	63

Hebrews

13:20	110

1 Peter

1:23	55
2:25	110
3:15	47
5:4	110